T0196973

Come On In
and Have Your
...Faith Lifted

The Torah-Like Wit & Wisdom
of Michael Franklin Ellis

EDITOR-IN-CHIEF: JOAN ELLIS SHATKIN

COMPILED AND ANNOTATED: DARCY F. WALLEN

BALBOA.
PRESS
A DIVISION OF HAY HOUSE

Balboa Press books may be ordered through
booksellers or by contacting:

Balboa Press
A Division of Hay House
1663 Liberty Drive
Bloomington, IN 47403
www.balboapress.com
1 (877) 407-4847

Because of the dynamic nature of the Internet, any web
addresses or links contained in this book may have changed
since publication and may no longer be valid. The views
expressed in this work are solely those of the author and do
not necessarily reflect the views of the publisher, and the
publisher hereby disclaims any responsibility for them.

The author of this book does not dispense medical advice or
prescribe the use of any technique as a form of treatment for
physical, emotional, or medical problems without the advice
of a physician, either directly or indirectly. The intent of the
author is only to offer information of a general nature to help
you in your quest for emotional and spiritual well-being. In
the event you use any of the information in this book for
yourself, which is your constitutional right, the author and
the publisher assume no responsibility for your actions.

Print information available on the last page.

ISBN: 978-1-5043-7213-8 (sc)
ISBN: 978-1-5043-7230-5 (e)

Library of Congress Control Number: 2016921282

Balboa Press rev. date: 09/11/2019

Contents

Foreword

My earliest, most colorful and unique memories of my grandfather, Michael Franklin Ellis, take me back to the 1950's and backyard family picnics, where brown paper candy sacks in his grasp, revealed large chocolate covered caramel lollipops made at one of Buffalo's finest confectioners. As the years progressed, at beloved family gatherings, grandchildren ran in circles around him while he recited witty poems and sang entertaining ditties. At family meals, he would mesmerize us with his tricks and antics, making bunny rabbits out of cloth napkins, 'accidently' banging into an opened door or blowing cigar smoke into drinking glasses turned upside down on the table. He always had an old fashioned song and a silly dance for us. During quiet moments, while sitting with the family, he would often reach into his chest shirt pocket, pull out the smallest paper pad and pencil and write down mysterious words, his "versifications," that would ultimately become poems, complex full pages of poetry, one liners, ballads and limericks.

He was proud of his children, grandchildren, and great-grandchildren. Along with his beloved wife, Corinne, whom he married in 1920, he planned summer picnics, holiday dinners and family vacations, to bask in his family's glow of vivid characters and intense energy that inspired so many of his poems.

Our grandfather was magical; from another place and time; born in 1897 in Buffalo, New York. He had such a way with words that he was the poet laureate of his high school senior class. As a young adult, he composed jingles and ad copy as the CEO of his own eponymous advertising agency.

The following pages will provide readers with a glimpse into this wonderful, talented and deeply spiritual man, Michael Franklin Ellis, whom we affectionately called "Gramp." Shortly before our mother's passing. My sister, Darcy, told her that she wanted to republish selected poems with religious content from Gramp's 13 self-published books. In support of the project, our mom requested that it be done through The TELLL Fund, which she helped us establish in our father Samuel Shatkin, DDS, MD's memory. Mom even put up the initial funds for the self-publishing package through Balboa Press (Hay House Publications). Once the poems were chosen, Darcy read them to our convalescing mother, one at a time. Familiar with so many of her father's poems, Mom would help "finish them up" while they were being read to her. Her non-verbal 'thumbs up,' 'thumbs down' or shrug-of-the-shoulders were the determining factors of which poems would finally go into this book. Thus, in essence, Mom, may her memory be blessed, is the editor-in-chief of this offering. The Jewish source materials in this book have been culled by and commented on by my dear sister, Darcy. Overall editing and guidance has come from Darcy's long time friend, Mashi, who has also been part of the project since its inception. We are grateful for the efforts of Darcy's team of Rabbis and friends who have brought this project to fruition.

It is our hope, that through this small book, you will be inspired and amazed by Gramp's intuitively Torah-like wisdom toward life.

Affectionately,
Cynthia E. Oppenheimer

Gramp's Namesake

MICHAEL F. ELLIS, III

I am proud to be the third person to carry the name of Michael Franklin Ellis Sr., our beloved "Gramp." I am the second-oldest of his 11 grandchildren, and as the son of his namesake Michael Franklin Ellis Jr., I was named Michael Franklin Ellis, III.

You have probably never met anyone as full of energy and zest for living as "Mike" was. He started every morning getting ready for his day while singing silly songs. He was always full of humor, energy and optimism. He was a brilliant man, a scholar even though he was not a college graduate. And what a public speaker! He could regale you with funny stories for hours on end.

He was a quietly religious man. I often heard him say things like, "The Lord takes such good care of me that I don't know how He has the time to take care of anyone else."

All of his children and grandchildren had so much fun just being in his company. His optimism and positive energy radiated out to envelop everyone around him. We are very lucky to be part of his family and we will always think of him with great love and respect.

A Tribute by Her Dear Friend

When I think of Joan Ellis Shatkin what comes to mind is a contemporary woman of valor. A remarkable person of many talents and great creativity in her work in advertising, in her leadership as national president of her sorority and first woman president of Temple Beth Zion. But she was more than the sum of these parts.

Her generous spirit supported community services and her warmth and understanding of people allowed her to be open and receptive to many new ideas. To Joan however, her family was her greatest joy. She delighted in her children, grandchildren and great grandchildren and their accomplishments. She was not only a caring wife and mother, but a giving daughter, sister, grandmother, and great-grandmother. In the true sense of the meaning of Eishes Chayil; Joan was giving to her family a source of stability and love that had to exceed all others.
Claire Goldberg

Acknowledgments and Gratitude

This is being published In memory of our dear mother, Joan Ellis April 28, 1930 - November 16, 2011

"Boruch Atoh...shehecheyanu, v'kiyimanu, v'higiyanu liz'man hazeh – Blessed are You Lord God, King of the Universe, who has granted us life, sustained us and enabled us to reach this occasion."
(Blessing for infrequent opportunities and special occasions)

First and foremost, I offer thanks to God above, Who has given me all that I have and enabled me to do all that I have the opportunity to do day-to-day. I feel so grateful to be able to facilitate the republication of a small collection of the wise and witty poetry of my dearly beloved grandfather, Michael Franklin Ellis, ob"m. I am so thankful to Hashem that He has placed me in my special family of birth that bequeaths this legacy.*

Throughout this project, the opportunity to reconnect with the one we call "Gramp" has been an incredibly enriching experience. I have been able to reminisce and be infused with Gramp's infectious positive energy. For quite a while, almost daily, as I pass his official portrait at the top of my staircase (see the back cover), I tell Gramp, "We're almost done with the book." Now finally, I can proudly say, "Here it is!" as I walk past his likeness.

This publication is in humble gratitude to, and in honor and memory of, my dear mother, Joan Ellis Shatkin (Chana bas Michoel, ob"m), who is the editor-in-chief as well as part sponsor and publisher of this book. After living away from home for close to 30 years, my husband, Eli (Louis) Wallen and I moved back almost a decade ago when my parents were becoming frail. After my father, ob"m passed away, my mother lost interest in her various pastimes and pleasures. To keep her distracted and happy, I would get her involved in many of my projects, which she loved and often lived vicariously through them. One such project was to start a fund with Buffalo's Foundation for Jewish Philanthropies in my father's (eventually my parents') name. My mother helped choose the acronym and title - TELLL Fund, Torah Experience for Life-Long Learning - and she requested that this book be a project of The TELLL Fund. Since her passing, The TELLL Fund has been a vehicle to enrich various parts of the Buffalo Jewish community, including helping school projects such as: giving a grant for a Jewish music program, funding a mitzvah curriculum, purchasing library books, helping two mikvahs with a blessing placard, providing free lectures, honorarium for speakers, evenings of inspiration, holistic wellness programs, entertainment and more. (Please see the page following these acknowledgments for the activities of the Fund in my parents' memory.)

I thank my mother for the motivation to develop The TELLL Fund, which is now in memory of both of our parents. May they look upon us from above and bless us with success, health and strength.

In considering how to format this book, I sifted through all of Gramp's books* and selected out those poems that sounded most Torah-like. Then, I brought them to my mother, the original editor-in-chief, and read them with her while she was convalescing in the skilled nursing facility in her complex, and then when she returned to her home. I can vividly see her in my mind's eye, giving a thumbs up to those poems which she approved of, thumbs down to those that she did not want to include. Many of the poems she chose are in this short volume. We have many more poems and thoughts of more books to come. Thus, this book is dedicated to Mom for being the impetus for this book, with which I have gained much pleasure. Thank you Mom, for the opportunity to connect again with your father, whose legacy we all share. Thank you Mom for sharing the

Ellis tradition of Judaism, communal service, joie de vivre, music, humor, language, culture, leadership and so much more!

A hearty thank you to my husband, Eliyohu Michoel (Louis) Wallen, who puts up with my crazy schedule and overexuberance for my projects. May he be able to put up with my schtick for many healthy, happy years and have nachas from my endeavors too!

Special thanks are due to my dear sister, Cynthia Ellen Oppenheimer (Cindy) who has helped The TELLL Fund and its projects since its inception and continues to support me in my creative endeavors. Thank you Cindy for being my best sister and for providing morale and the foreword to this volume.

There are not enough words to thank my dearest friend, colleague, collaborator and editor, Mashi Benzaquen, LCSW, who assisted me with this and other creative and therapeutic projects for publication and dissemination.

My continuous admiration and awe are due to Rabbi Yisroel Heshel Greenberg, who has afforded me an almost weekly opportunity to collect the treasures and bask in the warm lights of the Holy Torah, despite the 'cold' exile of Buffalo. Additionally, he has read through the manuscript of this volume, ascertaining that my source materials are accurate.

Additional thanks are due to: Deirdra Fox (Graphics), Leah Weintraub and Rivkah Lambert (Writing/Editing), Yehudis Chana Meshchaninov (Proofreading), Rabbis Yehoshua Greenberg, Betzalel Bassman, Zalman Nelson (Rabbinical Consultants), Michael F. Ellis, III (Biographical Integrity), Shira Goldberg (Interview of Mom for Gramp's Biography), Hanna Donner, Miriam Mitchell and Dana Kurtzman (clerical support). And, again, last but certainly not least, my dear sister Cindy, who has supported me in all of the TELLL Fund's amazing endeavors to provide Jewish cultural programming, educational materials and grants to Jewish organizations in Western New York.

---

*The poems were initially published by Gramp's business, Ellis Advertising Company. The poems in this book are being published by Toratherapeutics® and The TELLL Fund, in memory of Dr. and Mrs. Samuel Shatkin. See the Appendix for the document Gramp provided which grants me clear and direct permission to use his poetry in any way I deem appropriate as long as I ascribe it to his name – "My Legacy from Gramp."

For the Love of Mike is the title of the book I put out posthumously, in 1985, in my grandfather's memory. At the time, I contacted my cousins, aunts and uncles and parents and asked each of them for their favorite of Gramp's poems. See the Appendix for the cover to that book which was conceived by my mother, Joan Ellis Shatkin, ob"m. When I told her of that project, she was gung ho. The next morning, she told me she had a dream that her father came to her and told her what he wanted on the cover! "Put my portrait on the front and the family tree on the back" were Gramp's instructions to my mother from the next world! She was working for him even in his passing.

Darcy F. Wallen (a.k.a. Rus Devorah Wallen)

SUMMARY OF ACTIVITIES TO DATE

2010
TELLL Fund Community Memorial Lecture - Rabbi Y. H. Greenberg -
"Medicine & Torah"
TELLL Fund Women's Class - Rebbetzin Ronya Fajnland - *"Faith & Future"*

2011
TELLL Fund Yahrtzeit Memorial Lecture - Richard Sugarman, Ph.D.
"The Importance of Torah Education Today"
TELLL Fund Community Memorial Lectures - Roxanne Perri
"Saints & Sinners" and *"The Graphology of Relationships"*

2012
TELLL Fund Yahrtzeit Memorial Lecture - Steve & Judy Gerber -Sugarman, Esq.
"Remembering Aunt Joan"
Ohr Temimim School - Core Mitzvah Curriculum (year 1)
Mikvah of Buffalo Mikvah Blessing Sign in Hebrew/English Transliteration
TELLL Fund Women's Event - Rabbi Y. H. Greenberg - *"Healing and The Torah"*
Knesset Center/Chabad of Buffalo - Mikvah Blessing Sign
in Hebrew/English/Transliteration
Chabad House of Buffalo/Hillel of Buffalo -
Honorarium for Alan Veingrad Shabbaton
TELLL Fund Community Memorial Lecture - Roxanne Perri
"Secrets in the Garden of Graphology"

2013
Ohr Temimim School - Grant for Binding Machine for Educational Materials
Ohr Temimim School - Core Mitzvah Curriculum (year 2)
Ohr Temimim School - Donation of Library Books
Jewish Discovery Center - Grant for Educational Programming
TELLL Fund Community Event (at The JCC) -
"Saturday Night LIVE" with Reuven Russell
TELLL Fund Community Event (at The JCC) -
NOGA™ Holistic Women's Program
Chabad House of Buffalo - Honorarium for Esther Piekarski - *"Women In Judaism"*

2014
TELLL Fund Yahrtzeit Memorial Lecture - Rabbi Shloma Majeski -
"The Mystical Approach to Joy"
Chabad House of Buffalo - Honorarium for Tamir Goodman Shabbaton
Knesset Center/Chabad of Buffalo Honorarium for Rabbi Shea Hecht *"Cultbuster"*

2015
TELLL Fund Community Event - *"A Woman's Work of Heart and Soul"*
Ohr Temimim School - Grant for Jewish Music Program

2016
Ohr Temimim School Music Programs Implemented (in school and extracurricular)
TELLL Fund Yahrtzeit Memorial Event — Recital — Mikhoel Pais, pianist
TELLL Fund Book in Memory of Joan E. Shatkin (Projected) -
"Come On In And Have Your Faith Lifted"

"Gramp"

Now a bit about Michael Franklin Ellis, a.k.a. – "Gramp" and "Mike." Everyone who knew him considered him brilliant in every sense of the word. He shone brightly in every milieu; as a husband, father and grandfather, CEO of his own advertising company, cultural ambassador, poet laureate, humorist, orator, philanthropist, community activist, Jewish leader, and friend to all. We all knew him as "Gramp," others called him "Mike." We are all indebted to him for his impact on all our lives as cousins (grandchildren), parents and aunts and uncles.

Gramp was, and still remains an inspiration to all who knew him. He was always positive, optimistic, energetic, and kind...so very kind. Nana and Gramp were royalty in the truest sense of the word. They treated each other and everyone else with warmth and generosity. Dressing in style, wearing a top hat, sporting a walking stick, wearing gloves, driving his Rolls Royce, Gramp was the most regal man I ever knew. At the same time, he was very informal, fun and down to earth. I remember when he was already quite old, he would do a silly jig while singing a line such as, "When I was young I could sing and dance like this," then slowing down to a feeble walk, he'd say, "but now I can't do it anymore." When we were on cruises with our grandparents or at elegant banquets, Gramp would commence his antics by magically transforming cloth napkins into bunnies and trapping cigar smoke under water glasses, confusing the waiters and waitresses when they came back with our orders seeing the strange smoky overturned goblets. He was the most entertaining person to be around! He was also quite intuitive and knew each of our (eventual) personalities even when we were very young. He would summarize them in inscriptions to his 13 books that he gave to each of us annually for over a decade. (See the Appendix for some practically prophetic samples of inscriptions he wrote to me from when I was only between 2 and 5 years old!)

At Ellis Advertising he had a cadre of staff, eminently talented in their own specialized areas. Our dear mother, Joan Ellis Shatkin, ob"m, was the copy writer and editor. In those good old days, one of my favorite experiences was going downtown to work with my mother on the 17th floor of the Buffalo Statler-Hilton. When I was very young, my grandfather and mother so frequently called me "Darcy Dear," that I thought it was my real name. One day, when I was 4 or 5, on my way up the elevator to work with my mother and grandfather, a man asked me, "What is your name little girl," I answered, "Darcy Dear."* The whole elevator was full of chuckles while I was hopelessly clued out! I loved to go to Ellis Advertising and sit in on brainstorming sessions with my mother, Gramp and his creative team, where jingles and slogans, rhymes and graphic logo concepts were being proffered like a jazz riff. I am grateful for these special formative opportunities that have continued to enrich so much of my life.

Gramp was poised and regal. Even when relaxing in his study watching boxing and football, or writing his poetry, he would be smoking his pipes, filled with Borkum Riff aromatic cherry tobacco, while sporting his burgundy smoking jacket. These are my most cherished and vivid memories of Gramp from the end of his life when I had the unique opportunity to clean his pipes for him and assist him on his last publication, <u>A Book Of Rare Poems - Rare, Because They're Not Well Done</u>.* This was the finale of 13 books of humorous and philosophical poems he wrote and published under Ellis Advertising Company where he was owner and CEO. He went into work every day beginning in 1924 almost until his passing in 1984.

Having had the honor of putting together this volume, I have seen Gramp in a light in which none of us could have possibly envisioned. He had no formal training in this area as a *Talmid*

Chochom - A Torah scholar (literally in the Holy Tongue, "a wise student"). Reading all of Gramp's 13 books of poetry to select the verses quoted in this book as per my mother's request, I saw a side of Gramp that was remarkably, intuitively Torah-aligned, and more closely Chassidic in perspective. Seeing these verses from a totally different angle was quite miraculous for me.

As a youngster I had many questions about Judaism. During college, I was fortunate to meet a Lubavitcher Rabbi on my college campus, who was the first person to finally answer my questions with substance. That was the beginning of my Chassidic journey. Now I call myself an ever "Aspiring Lubavitcher." Revisiting these poems 35 years later, I am continuously amazed at Gramp's intuitive, Torah-like, Kabbalistic and Chassidic bent. I'm sure you will be in awe at the similarity too, as you read through this book and see the parallel Torah quotations we have included herein.

Most of Gramp's poems are witty and philosophical; some are outright sarcastic or sardonic. It was to the latter, more negative and "critical" poems (the Torah tradition would call these mussar-style), Mom gave a thumb's down. In life, she always glossed over the negative and put on a positive spin. When I shared this 'genre' with her, she wanted nothing of the sort in the book. From the verses contained in this book you will see how Gramp's humor and personality shine through them with wit and wisdom in the upbeat style of the clever, Chassidic aphorism. Thank you for reading thus far. I hope you will enjoy these pages. Please share your comments with me at: TELLLFund@gmail.com

Darcy F. Wallen (a.k.a. Rus Devorah Wallen), granddaughter of Michael Franklin Ellis, ob"m and daughter of Joan Ellis Shatkin ob"m and Dr. Samuel Shatkin, DDS, MD, ob"m.

---

* See appendix for book covers, dedications, inscriptions and graphics from his books, as well as a glossary of Hebrew, Aramaic and Yiddish terms found in this book.

CHAPTER 1

FAITH LIFT: TRUST IS A MUST

FAITH LIFTING

The sign on a temple whose
Rabbi quite gifted
Read, "Come on in and have
your faith lifted."

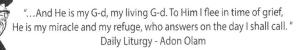

"…And He is my G-d, my living G-d. To Him I flee in time of grief,
He is my miracle and my refuge, who answers on the day I shall call. "
Daily Liturgy - Adon Olam

Chapter 1

FAITH LIFT: TRUST IS A MUST

...And He is my G-d, my living G-d. To Him I
flee in time of grief,
He is my miracle and my refuge, who
answers on the day I shall call.
At the time that I sleep and when I awake,
And with my soul and body G-d is with me, I
shall not fear."
Daily Liturgy - Adon Olam

FAITH LIFTING
The sign on a temple whose Rabbi quite gifted,
Read, "Come in and pray,
And you'll have your faith lifted."

FEAR NAUGHT
Fear naught in life save conscience,
That constant pricking prod.
For peace of mind obey it,
The still small voice of God.

NOT SEEING IS BELIEVING
Faith is that quality you will agree
When you believe in what you do not see.

WASTED WORRY
Worry's like a rocking chair
Neither gets you anywhere.

KEEP THE FAITH
Without faith man produces naught
While with faith greatest things are wrought.

FAITH LIFTED
If into the slough of despond you have drifted,
This moment's the right time to have your
faith lifted.

Judging from the volume of words that Ellis wrote about the concepts of *bitachon* (trust) and *emunah* (faith) – two Hebrew words that are often used interchangeably, we highlighted what was likely his favorite theme, and also the one that is most fundamentally Jewish. In these poems, only a fraction of which are presented here, Ellis explicitly and often mentions faith and God.

The following story illustrates the subtle yet significant difference between the two:

In November 1966, Mr. Benzion Rader, a Lubavitcher chassid was in a private audience with the Lubavitcher Rebbe. The Rebbe asked Mr. Rader if he knew what emunah meant.

Mr. Rader replied, "Emunah means faith, belief, and trust."

The Rebbe probed further, asking, "Do you know what bitachon is?"

Mr. Rader replied in the negative.

The Rebbe said, "If one is confronted with a problem and one has emunah, then one has faith, belief, and trust that God will help you overcome the problems. But if you have bitachon, you do not see that there is a problem because God does not send any problems--only challenges!"

"Bitachon is not baseless optimism. It does not mean, "Everything will be okay." Bitachon is trust in Hashem's kindliness and in His boundless mercy, understanding that it is the Creator's Will that we place our trust in His kindness. Therefore, we look to the future calmly and serenely, secure in the knowledge that we can rely on Him now and always."
- Nachmanides' (RaMbaN) Commentary on The Psalms

"Cast your burden upon Hashem and He will sustain you."
- Psalms 55:23

The Gate of Trust tells us the many benefits bitachon One *of them is, "This brings one to menuchas hanefesh – "peace of mind."*
- <u>Chovos HaLevavos – Duties of the Heart</u> by Ibn Pakuda at the beginning of the Sha'ar HaBitachon (The Gate of Trust)

"...The obligation to trust in G-d – to have Bitachon – is not merely to believe in G-d's ability to treat one benevolently and to rescue him from distress and the like. It means that one trusts that G-d will in fact do this. And this trust is so certain that the individual is completely relaxed and not worried in the slightest. This is spelled out in Chovos HaLevavos: "One who trusts in G-d has a tranquil spirit. His heart relies on the One in Whom he has placed his trust."
- <u>In Good Hands – 100 Letter and Talks of the Lubavitcher</u> <u>Rebbe, on Bitachon: Trusting in God,</u> Compiled and Translated by Uri Kaploun

FACE THE BAND
If you can face life's problems
And keep things well in hand,
If you can face the music,
You may someday lead the band.

Gam zu l'tova is a popular Jewish expression that means: "This too is for the best." No matter what happens, no matter how it first appears, ultimately, everything God does is for the best.

The Talmud tells of a famous Jewish character named Nachum of Gamzu who excelled in the quality of *bitachon*. No matter what difficulties befell him, Nachum of Gamzu always said, "*Gam zu l'tova* - This too is for the best!"

In this story, God makes a lifesaving miracle for Nachum of Gamzu:

Once, the Jews desired to send the Emperor a gift - and after discussing who should go, they decided that Nachum of Gamzu should go because he had experienced many miracles. They sent him with a bag full of precious stones and pearls.

Nachum of Gamzu went and spent the night in a certain inn and during the night the people in the inn arose and emptied the bag and filled it up with earth. When he discovered this next morning he exclaimed, "This also is for the best."

When he arrived at his destination and they undid his bag, they found that it was full of earth. The king thereupon desired to put them all to death saying, "The Jews are mocking me." Nachum then exclaimed, "This also is for the best."

Whereupon Elijah appeared in the guise of one of them and remarked, "Perhaps this is some of the earth of their father Abraham, for when he threw earth [against the enemy], it turned into swords and when [he threw] stubble it changed into arrows, for it is written, 'His sword makes them as dust, his bow as the driven stubble.'"

Now there was one province which [the emperor had hitherto] not been able to conquer, but when they tried some of this earth [against it] they were able to conquer it. Then they took him [Nachum] to the royal treasury and filled his bag with precious stones and pearls and sent him back with great honor.

When on his return journey he again spent the night in the same inn he was asked, "What did you take [to the king] that they showed you such great honor?" He replied, "I brought there what I had taken from here."

[The innkeepers] thereupon razed the inn to the ground and took of the earth to the king and they said to him, "The earth that was brought to you belonged to us. They tested it and it was not found to be [effective] and the innkeepers were thereupon put to death."
- The Talmud, Tractate Ta'anis 21a

"Genuine trust means putting our entire confidence in God and remembering Him in every detail of our activities, being aware that no matter what we may attempt, success depends not on what we do, but only on the will of God."
- Rabbeinu Bachaye in Kad HaKemach

*"Is G-d really in need of your worry as to how
He is going to run your affairs and solve your
problems? Or will He succeed in finding good
solutions even without your worrying?"*
- In Good Hands – 100 Letters and Talks of The
Lubavitcher Rebbe, on Bitachon: Trusting in God,
Compiled and Translated by Uri Kaploun

HAVE TRUST WILL TRAVEL
I bring to you an axiom
That points a simple story,
The day you have your faith and trust
You'll promptly lose each worry.

"Kindness surrounds one who trusts in Hashem."
- Tehillim 32:10

King David clearly promises that Divine goodness
always accompanies a person who trusts in the
Creator of the world.

"But as for me, I trust in Your kindness."
- Psalms, 13:6

Rabbi Shmuel of Lubavitch called the "Rebbe
Maharash," used to say, *"L'chatchila ariber."* This
means that many people in the world think that
when one is faced with a problem or obstacle, one
should try to go around it or avoid it. However the
Rebbe Maharash said that one should "in the first
instance go right over it." If it stands in the way
of serving God it is merely an imaginary obstacle
and one should a priori, go over it.

REVERSES
When you're kicked in the rear
Like a football punt
Don't worry it proves
That you're out in front.

COUNT YOUR BLESSINGS
The little man
Who always loses
Counts not his blessings
But his bruises.

FACE THE MUSIC WITH A SONG
When the nurses in the clinic
Have placed you in the cart
And it's time to face the music
Let a song be in your heart.

"Beyond faith: The ability to exercise self-control eliminates anxiety as it moves us beyond faith and into trust. The difference is profound. We can have faith that things will work out, but may still be plagued by worry and fleeting moments of doubt. When we have trust, however, negative thoughts do not fill our mind. We do not dwell on, or worry about, the outcome. Trust is an intellectual process, which is the natural outgrowth of our positive choices, and exists independent of our mood or emotional state."

-If God Were Your Therapist, Dovid Lieberman, Ph.D., p. 60

CHAPTER 2

WHAT YOU THINK ABOUT YOU BRING ABOUT

A VISION

You won't develop eye strain
This statement's bona fide
If when you look at life you
Will see the brighter side.

"Tracht Gut Vet Zein Gut - Think Good, It Will Be Good."
Rabbi(s) Menachem Mendel of Lubavitch

CHAPTER 2

WHAT YOU THINK ABOUT
YOU BRING ABOUT

"Tracht Gut Vet Zein Gut - Think Good, It Will Be Good."
Rabbi(s) Menachem Mendel of Lubavitch – Chabad Aphorism

BRIGHTER IS RIGHTER
The bright side of life
Is the right side of life.

OPTIMIST VS. PESSIMIST
The pessimist when he says "Howdy,"
Looks up and adds, "It's partly cloudy."
Contrary-wise (and this is funny)
The optimist says, "Partly sunny."

ASKING FOR TROUBLE?
When you invite trouble
You're hitting new depths
For when trouble's invited
It always accepts.

DON'T EVEN THINK OF IT...
"To get rid of a worry
On this point reflect
Pay it no attention
Then 'twill die of neglect."

MAKE UP YOUR MIND
Most men are as happy,
To that degree,
That they make up their minds
They are going to be.

STRIDE INTO THE SUNSET
I fear not the future
The Lord's on my side
As into the sunset
I buoyantly stride.

A VISION
You won't develop eye strain
This statement's bona fide
If when you look at life you
Will see the brighter side.

By encouraging positive thinking in his readers,
Ellis connects to the deep Jewish idea that
positive thinking impacts the world. A sound
spiritual practice includes the recognition and
awareness that everything comes from God and
that everything God does is ultimately for the
best. Ellis' poems direct us to focus not on the
"bruises" but on the "blessings." Look for and

focus your attention on the positive elements in every situation, and assume the best.

In Yiddish there is a saying: "Tracht Gut Vet Zein Gut," which means, "Think good and it will be good." The Lubavitcher Rebbe says that this is a promise.
- The Lubavitcher Rebbe in <u>Igros Kodesh</u> – Letters vol. 8, p. 358.

"Delight in the Lord, and He will give you what your heart desires."
- Psalms 37:4

"Commit your affairs to the Lord, and your plans will be established."
- Proverbs 16:3

"All physicians are in agreement that a joyful and happy state of mind increases physical, mental and spiritual health and wellbeing and assists the healing process."
- <u>Healthy in Body, Mind and Spirit, vol. 3</u> - Based on the Teachings of the Lubavitcher Rebbe, *Rabbi Menachem M. Schneerson*

Someone had begged him (the Third Lubavitcher Rebbe) *to intercede in order to arouse Heaven's mercies upon a patient who was dangerously ill. The Tzemach Tzekek replied: "Tracht gut vet zein gut - Think positively and things will be positive." This implies that the very fact of thinking positively*

— having trust — will give rise to results that are visibly and manifestly good.

This teaching may be understood as follows:
The obligation to place one's trust in God (to have bitachon) is not merely a component and a corollary of one's faith (emunah) that everything is in His hands and that He is gracious and compassionate. Such an obligation would not need to be stated separately. Rather, the obligation to place one's trust in God is an avodah of its own, an independent challenge in one's Divine service. That challenge is to rely on God to the point that one casts one's lot entirely into His hands — as in the verse "Cast your burden upon God" — and to be without any other support in the world apart from Him. It could well be that this is what the author of Chovos HaLevavos (Duties of the Heart) had in mind when he wrote that a person who has trust is "like a bondman who is incarcerated in a dungeon on the authority of his master." That prisoner's trust is beamed only toward his master, "to whose hands he is subordinate, and no man but him can bring harm or help."

POSITIVELY
I've found the 'confidentest' of all men
He does his crossword puzzles with a pen.

WHAT'S EATING YOU?
Here's food for thought
With you in view
Don't be consumed

By what's eating you.

The Lubavitcher Rebbe often spoke of how thinking good, reinforced by a trust in G-d, is just as important to the healing process as medicine and doctors. In 1977, the Rebbe suffered a serious heart attack. One day later, he insisted on giving a talk, as he had done on that particular day for the previous 38 years. *"You must take care of your health"* the doctor insisted. *"If not, there is a twenty-five percent chance of a relapse."*

The doctor asked if the Rebbe understood what he had said. *"Oh, yes,"* said the Rebbe with a smile. *"You said that even if I don't take care of my health -- which, I assure you, I will -- there is a seventy-five percent chance that there won't be a relapse."*

BIRTH OF A NOTION
Every new idea is
The subject of much scorn.
And sneered at as impossible
Until it has been born.

RAYS
Those pessimists,
Who make me fume,
Absorb sunshine,
Then give forth gloom.

THE PESSIMIST
The pessimist gets all shook up,
Begins to growl and pout,

When you tell him in soothing tones,
"There's naught to fret about."

NOT TOO BRIGHT
On the bright side of life,
He will not focalize,
For he says the bright side,
Is bad for his eyes.

"CAN'T"- ERBURY TALES
When little boys
Say, "no" perchance,
The best cure is
A kick in the can'ts.

PROPHESY
If you can greet each new tomorrow,
With joy, withstanding every sorrow;

If you can smile when things go wrong.
And not collapse but come back strong;

Of life then you'll enjoy the best,
From day of birth, 'til day of rest.

CHAPTER 3

TRUE WEALTH: BEYOND THE BANK ACCOUNT

THE REAL ESTATE

On this point I could write
A most pleasant sonnet.
What e'er your "lot" in life
Just be sure to build on it.

"Eizeh hu ha oshir ha same'ach b'chelko
Who is wealthy? He who is satisfied with his portion."
Ethics of the Fathers - 4:1

CHAPTER 3

TRUE WEALTH:
BEYOND THE BANK ACCOUNT

"Eizeh hu ha oshir ha same'ach b'chelko
Who is wealthy? He who is satisfied with his
portion."
Ethics of the Fathers - 4:1

START COUNTING
Your blessings count,
If you'd sleep well
For thoughts unhappy
They dispel.

LESS TROUBLE
Compare your griefs with others
And this is my guess,
You will find that your troubles
Are less, yes, far less.

COMPARE THEM
Compare your griefs with other men
And you will find they'll seem less crucial.

While others weigh theirs by the ton,
Yours may be weighed but by the bushel.

Hakaras Hatov; in Judaism, the ability to recognize and acknowledge good, is a highly regarded trait. Since our tradition teaches us that even when the opposite appears true everything God sends us ultimately for our good. We are taught to thank Him even for the troubles He sends us. Our troubles are tailor-made, often to bring out our strengths and dormant qualities. Being grateful, both for our obvious blessings *and* for our challenges, is a fundamental Jewish value.

A disciple of Rabbi Dov Ber, the Maggid of Mezeritch, once asked his Rebbe for help with a difficulty he was having. *"The Talmud instructs us 'to bless G-d for the bad in our life just as we bless Him for the good,' but is such a level really possible? How can someone have the same reaction, the same gratitude, to suffering and joy?"*

"Go see Reb Zusha of Anipoli, my disciple," said Rabbi Dov Ber.

Arriving at Reb Zusha's house, the man was received warmly and invited to make himself at home. *"I'll observe his conduct before asking the question,"* thought the man. And it very quickly became clear that Reb Zusha truly exemplified the Talmudic instruction he found so challenging. He couldn't think of anyone who suffered more hardships than Reb Zusha: poverty, starvation, afflictions, and illnesses. But in the entire time he spent with Reb Zusha, the man never saw him be anything but positive full of gratitude.

"How does he do it?" wondered the man, and he resolved to ask his host. *"I want to ask you something, which in fact is the whole reason I'm here. Our Rebbe told me to ask you."*

The visitor repeated the question he had asked the Maggid: *"How can someone have the same reaction, the same gratitude, to suffering and joy?"*

"You raise a good point," said Reb Zusha, after thinking the matter through. *"But why did our Rebbe send you to me? How would I know? He should have sent you to someone who has experienced suffering."*

A person is obligated to bless G-d for the bad just as he blesses Him for the good, as it is written: *"And you shall love the Lord your G-d with all your heart, with all your soul, and with all your might."*
- Talmud, Tractate Brochos 54a

THE HAPPY MAN
A man whose small wants he enjoys is happier indeed
Than he who ever cries for more and always is in need.

In a world driven by material aspirations, Ellis firmly believed in being content with what we already have. This attitude offers true blessing and satisfies us more deeply than acquiring shiny new objects. According to Jewish tradition, there is no end to wanting; joy is found in being happy with what we already have.

Who is rich? One who is satisfied with his lot; as is stated: *"If you eat of the toil of your hands, fortunate are you, and good is to you."*
- Psalm 128:2

"Fortunate are you" in this world "and good is to you" in the World to Come.
- Ethics of the Fathers 4:1

No one is poorer than he who is not satisfied with his lot.
- Mivchar Hapnimim 46, R. Solomon ibn Gabirol, 11th century Spanish rabbi, Jewish philosopher and poet

I LOVE MY LOT
My lot in life
Would be just what
I'd love; if I
But had a "lot."

Many Jewish teachings highlight the futility of the quest for monetary wealth, particularly as an end in itself. The teachings also emphasize the downside of the desire for physical possessions, the problems that go along with owning much, as well as the importance of being satisfied with what we have.

"One who increases possessions, increases worry."
- Ethics of the Fathers 2:7

"Whoever loves silver will not be sated with silver."
 - Ecclesiastes 5:9

"One who has a hundred wants two hundred; one who has two hundred wants four hundred."
- Midrash Koheles Raba (Ecclesiastes) 1:13

"There is one who appears rich but has nothing; one who appears poor but has great wealth."
- Proverbs 13:7

"Generally those who chase after money end up in debt and are left with nothing. Even if they aren't literally in debt, they are indebted [subjugated] to the lust of their soul [that constantly wants more]. They put themselves in crazy, dangerous situations in order to acquire more and more."
- Likkutei Moharan 23:5, Rebbe Nachman of Breslov (1772-1810)

"Lacking numerous possessions is not bad; worrying about not having them is bad."
- Torei HaYogon 13, Shem Tov ben Ibn Plekira
Spanish Rabbi, philosopher and poet (1225-1295)

THE REAL ESTATE
On this point I could write
A most pleasant sonnet.
What e'er your "lot" in life
Just be sure to build on it.

In Judaism, as with other faith traditions, attaining spiritual riches is more valued than seeking material abundance. No matter the gifts we're endowed with at birth, we are only considered successful if we continue to grow. We must constantly advance intellectually, spiritually and emotionally, or else we stagnate and lose ground.

Through this series of poems, Ellis emphasizes that being happy with what we have is in itself a source of happiness, versus yearning for that which we do not have, which brings out the traits of worry, jealousy, frustration and even greed. When we accept and trust that God is the provider of all for all, we also trust that everything we have right now is everything we need; and thus, we are happy.

CHAPTER 4

LIGHTEN UP TO BRIGHTEN UP!

LIGHT VERSE

Here is an admonition it
Will pay each one to hark;
To light a candle's easier than
To execrate the dark.

"M'at min ha'or docheh harbeh min ha choshech
A Little Light Dispels Much Darkness."
Rabbi Schneur Zalman of Liadi

CHAPTER 4

LIGHTEN UP!

M'at min ha'or docheh harbeh min ha choshech - A little light dispels much darkness."
Rabbi Schneur Zalman of Liadi

WATER JOY
Getting into hot water
May make you feel mean
But you'll find it's the best way
To keep yourself clean.

THE HURDLES
Thank God for the problems
That stand in our way;
They cause us to fight to
O'ercome them each day.

Yisaron ha'or min ha choshech is usually translated as, "There is an advantage of light to darkness." However, the more literal translation as well as Chassidic and mystical explanation is as follows:

The literal translation of the phrase is, "...an advantage of light **from** the darkness." Mystically, the verse means that there is an advantage of light **from out of** the darkness itself! It is not simply by contrast to it in the typical translation of the "advantage of light **over** folly." When we go through challenges in our lives, that which we gain and learn in the process catapults us to a level that is much higher than if we had never fallen in the first place. Therefore, there is an advantageous aspect to the "light" that comes from the difficult experience, because we have proactively and consciously made new efforts with a greater, stronger energy than was previously available. Similarly, by way of analogy, the squeezing of the olive produces the oil that illuminates.

"It's the darkness that brings the light [not just by way of demonstration], but actually when one has darkness – obstacles, that can cause him to become stronger."
- Or HaTorah Bamidbar Vol., 1 p. 269, Tzemach Tzedek

"Even when God is in hiding, we are not helpless. We can increase in Divine light, which brings real, palpable joy. Joy gives strength to break out of barriers and obstructions [on all levels] in one's personal life, in society, in the darkness of exile."
- The Lubavitcher Rebbe, Rabbi Menachem M. Schneerson

THE CURVE THAT STRAIGHTENS
A smile is a curve that will dissipate
All troubles you have, and will set them straight.

SWEET MUSIC
A smile in conversation –
(And I know I am not wrong)
Will brighten up the wordings
As a melody does a song.

THE DEFLATER
No diet can reduce the head that's fat.
Adversity alone takes care of that.

LIGHT VERSE
Here is an admonition it
Will pay each one to hark;
To light a candle's easier than
To execrate the dark.

PASTE IT ON
Keep smiling and then
You'll soon see
You can be as happy
As you want to be.

According to the principles of *emuna* (faith), defined as the belief that God looks after each person in a uniquely personalized fashion, our problems and challenges are not random. Rather, they are designed for us to overcome and to help us grow. The greater the obstacle, the greater the energy that is required to overcome it. This brings out unrevealed strengths in a person who can now achieve more and bring more light into the world through his growth.

LIVE AND LIVE AGAIN
No death there is,
Naught ever dies,
What's now decay,
Once more will rise.

BEGINNING AGAIN
Just as the sun must shine,
Then too must come the rain.
So life is meant to cease,
And to begin again.

We come into this world as incomplete beings. Our mission in life is to make a *tikkun* (rectification) to correct our *middos* (traits), our personal character flaws, and thereby perfect our souls.

The concept of reincarnation, the idea that what lives today has lived before and will live again on this earth, is deeply rooted in Jewish sources. Souls that rotate through different lives in this world are called *gilgulim*.

We may experience several incarnations in order to complete our rectification. Facing our trials and tribulations with the idea that they are our pathway to elevation and redemption causes us to strive for excellence and never give in to despair.

"Reincarnation may be necessary to complete rectification of all aspects of each level of the soul."
-Shabtai Teicher's commentary on <u>Sha'ar Hagilgulim</u> by Rabbi Yitzchak Luria (The Arizal)

"All pure and holy spirits live on in heavenly places, and in the course of time they are again sent down to inhabit righteous bodies."
- Josephus. Jewish historian. 1st Century C.E.

CHAPTER 5

BETTER NOW THAN EVER

THIS VERY MINUTE

Do a kindness now
And do not hesitate;
Tomorrow you may find
Will be a day too late.

"V'im lo achshav, aimasai? If not now, when?"
Ethics of the Fathers - 1:14

CHAPTER 5

BETTER NOW THAN EVER

"V'im lo achshav, aimasai?
If not now, when?"
Ethics of the Fathers - 1:14

DON'T LOOK BACK
Never look back-
wards or you may
Miss what's coming
To you today.

In Genesis (24:1), it says, "And Abraham was old and on in years." However, the literal translation of the words is "coming with days – *ba b'yamim*." One explanation is that when one lives life to the fullest, living truly in the present each moment, one is efficient and productive as well - not dwelling on the future or past. Just as when Abraham was old, he came with his all of his days testifying on his behalf because of his full life from living in the moment.

The world says, 'Time is money.' I say, 'Time is life.'
- The Lubavitcher Rebbe to Mr. Gershon Ber Jacobson in 1985.

"In each journey of your life you must be where you are. You may only be passing through on your way to somewhere else seemingly more important - nevertheless, there is a purpose in where you are right now."
 - The Lubavitcher Rebbe, Rabbi Menachem M. Schneerson

Unfortunately many people are careless with their time; they waste it in frivolities...If one were to think about it he would realize how much time is worth. If one were to tell you are going to die on a certain date and for a certain amount of money you can live an extra day, man would pay anything for that extra day...
- Yaros Devash Vol. 2 p. 79b [Levuv 5623], R. Yonatan Eybeschutz, Talmudist, Halachist, Kabbalist, Rabbi of Prague and author (1690-1764)

TOO BUSY
He was too busy in the trade
To see me very often.
My visit now he can't evade
As he lies in his coffin.

Ellis understands the importance of taking time for rest and rejuvenation. One of the Ten Commandments is to rest on the seventh day:

"Remember the Sabbath day to sanctify it. Six days may you work and perform all your labor, but the seventh day is a Sabbath to the Lord, your God; you shall perform no labor... and He rested on the seventh day. Therefore, the Lord blessed the Sabbath day and sanctified it."
- Exodus 20:8-11

BIG THINGS – SMALL PACKAGES
If you would succeed
In our world of today
Do every small thing
In a really big way.

LIVING-GIVING
To his age the best gift
That a man can be giving
Is a life of the fullest
And most creative living.

Here, Ellis is teaching us to pay attention to the way we expend our efforts and creative gifts. It's important to "have one's head in the game" and not to coast through life expending as little effort as possible. Regardless of what we hope to accomplish, effort, even in small matters, is crucial. Additionally, staying cognizant that our time is limited and that we must take advantage of each moment is a value that Ellis lived in his own life, moment to moment.

LIVING IN THE MOMENT
The present I'm fully enjoying
Though the journey be smooth or be rough
I give little thought to the future
For it will be here soon enough.

"Grant it that life, and this moment will endure forever. Fail to do so, and it has already left, as a moment that never was."
- The Lubavitcher Rebbe, Rabbi Menachem M. Schneerson

"One time, my father-in-law, the (Previous) Rebbe, was scheduled to travel from Leningrad to Moscow on secret business concerning his underground network. Such a journey was fraught with peril, especially because his movements were closely monitored by the communist authorities. However, when I entered his room shortly before his departure, I found him sitting in a state of utter calm, as if nothing urgent were on the horizon. When I expressed my amazement, the Rebbe explained: "You cannot add time to the day, but you can utilize the time you do have 'successfully.'" When one is fully engaged in the moment – not distracted by that which came before, or that which will come after – then he is truly living and is able to utilize life's potential to its fullest."

Rabbi Menachem M. Schneerson - Sefer Hasichos, 5700 (book of talks by the Lubavitcher Rebbe) pp. 113-4

-Sefer Hasichos, 5700 (book of talks by the Lubavitcher Rebbe) pp. 113-4

The Rebbe Rayatz (Rabbi Yosef Yitzchok Schneersohn, sixth Chabad Rebbe, 1880-1950) offers this advice on completing both small and big actions in a proper way: *"He accomplished so much and had success with time by doing each act calmly and patiently. When you do things calmly, it makes you more efficient in the long term."*
- Sefer Hasichos, 5700 (book of talks by the Lubavitcher Rebbe) pp. 113-4

THIS VERY MINUTE
Do a kindness now
And do not hesitate;
Tomorrow you may find
Will be a day too late.

The Mitzvah of counting the Omer is to count the days from Passover until Shavuos, when the Omer offering was brought in the Temple. This Mitzvah is puzzling, as we normally count things to determine if we have lost anything or whether we should add or subtract to what we have. The one thing in the world that a person cannot lose, add to or subtract from, is time. Why do we count something that we cannot control? Each day has a purpose. Whether it leads up to the Omer offering or it is an ordinary day of life, we must look at the clock, and ask ourselves, "Am I using my time properly, to fulfill my mission in this world?"

- From a Talk of The Lubavitcher Rebbe, Rabbi
Menachem M. Schneerson, 11 Nissan 5742 - April
04, 1982

*"Don't push it off till tomorrow, lest there won't
be a morrow."*
- Proverbs 27:1

*"The Baal Shem Tov teaches that at every single
moment all of existence is created anew from
nothingness. So, if at this moment one has the
opportunity to achieve good, and a moment later
the world will revert to utter nothingness and will
need to be created again – should he wait to make
things right?"*
-From a Talk of The Lubavitcher Rebbe, Rabbi
Menachem M. Schneerson, 10 Kislev 5748 -
December 1, 1987

REAPING REWARD
Here's an old proverb
As true as can be
If you'd eat the fruit
You must climb the tree.

ACTION ABOVE ALL
Ideas are
The things it's true
That never work
Unless you do.

PAIN FOR GAIN
Were there no pains

There'd be no gains.

GET BUSY
By this old adage I will swear
In idleness there bides despair.

Through these poems, Ellis emphasizes the importance of effort to achieve our goals. The Hebrew word for laziness is *atzlus*. Many Jewish teachings warn against laziness and encourage people to work toward their goals.

"Through laziness the rafter sinks, and with idleness of the hands the house leaks."
- Ecclesiastes, 10:18

"God does not dwell amongst laziness."
- Talmud (Shabbos 30b) quoting Rav Yehuda ben Shmuel

"Love labor; do not stop working, idleness brings to weariness, this is the defect of laziness...When one stops working [for a while], when he will need to get back to it, his body will push back [and not want to work] for habit controls the body...One thinks that not working will give him peace and calmness, the opposite is true, when he stops working [out of laziness] working becomes that much more difficult..."
- Commentary to Pirkei Avos 1:11, Rabbeinu Yonah (R. Yonah ben Abraham Gerondi), Spanish scholar (d. 1263)

I LOST AN HOUR
In the morn I lost an hour.
All day long I searched for it.
If a hundred years I'd scour,
I'd recover not a whit.

Ellis reminds us of the futility of wasting time and the inability to recapture what has already passed. The Jewish concept of *bitul zman* refers to wasting time that could have been devoted to loftier purposes.

In his book <u>Portrait of a Chassid: The Life and Legacy of</u> <u>Rabbi Zvi Hirsch Gansbourg</u>, Rabbi Simon Jacobson tells the following story about a talk the Lubavitcher Rebbe gave on a Shabbat afternoon. The Rebbe spoke for close to an hour and several times during his talk, he was moved to tears. He explained the verse: *"I shall fill the number of your days"* (Exodus 23:26) in the following way:

"God grants every person a fixed number of days to complete his Divine service.... This applies not only to the days; even the hours and minutes are accounted for and a person must [use] every moment to the fullest. This point should constantly be gnawing at a person; he should feel under strain and under pressure, contemplating what he could be doing to use this moment fully."

LOST
Some men get lost in thought, like lost in space
Because thought is an unfamiliar place.

HERE TODAY
Oh, how I love the sun
Each burning ray;
It proves that I'm alive
Another day.

RAILROADED
Oh stop, look and listen
Ere you cross the track,
For should you not do so
You may not come back.

Whether Ellis was being lighthearted about what can happen if we don't pay attention to a train moving down the track, or philosophical about having an appreciation for natural beauty, he reminds us to be mindful and grounded in the present moment.

Meditation is increasingly used as a therapeutic tool to achieve peace of mind and to become more "present." Judaism is not adverse to this as it is a mitzvah (commandment) to maintain good health. Therefore, if meditation can heal the physical, it is encouraged.

However, to be consistent with Jewish teachings, mediation is to be approached in a careful manner as some popular forms of meditation today...

stem directly from Eastern religions with all their overtones of idol worship. Does this mean that Jews must renounce any form of meditation? Not at all! The objection is not to meditation per se, but to the religious trappings, which invariably accompany contemporary meditational techniques. Judaism requires a healthy body and mind, and if everyday living is too full of stress and strain, then one may turn to meditation as an acceptable solution."

- The Lubavitcher Rebbe on Meditation

CHAPTER 6

A FRIEND IN DEED IS A FRIEND INDEED

MY FRIEND

My friend knows all about me,
What I will do and say.
He sees me as the man I am
And likes me anyway.

"V'ohavto l'reacho k'mocho - Love your fellow as yourself."
Leviticus 19:18

CHAPTER 6

A FRIEND IN DEED IS
A FRIEND INDEED

"V'ohavto l'reacho k'mocho -
Love your fellow as yourself."
Leviticus 19:18

A JEWEL
A friend is one who proves a jewel
When of yourself you've made a fool.

MY FRIEND
My friend knows all about me,
What I will do and say.
He sees me as the man I am
And likes me anyway.

FALSE FRIENDS
False friends are those who love us
When days are bright and gay,
But leave us with abandon
When skies turn dull and gray.

PUT IT ON THICK
Where love gives
God lives.
Where love is thin
Faults creep in.

ETERNAL MESSAGE
No favors for yourself request
That you'd not ask for others.
And idle hours are e'er spent best
In succoring your brothers.

Loyalty and faithfulness to others is so important in Judaism that we traditionally bless a newly-married couple that they should merit to build a faithful home in Israel *(bayis ne'eman b'Yisroel)*. Among other things, to be a loyal friend means overlooking the occasional mistakes our friends make as well as continuing to support a friend when the chips are down.

The Mishnah says, *"Any love that is dependent on something –– when the thing ceases, the love also ceases. But a love that is not dependent on anything, never ceases. What is [an example of] a love that is dependent on something? It is the love of Amnon for Tamar. And one that is not dependent on anything? It is the love of David and Jonathan."*
- Ethics of the Fathers 5:16

"Anyone who establishes a friendship for access to power, money, or sexual relations; when these

*ends are not attainable, the friendship ceases...
"love that is not dependent on selfish ends is
true love of the other person since there is no
intended end."*
- Rabbi Shimon ben Tzemach Duran (Spain, North
Africa 14th-15th century) <u>Magen Avot</u> – (abridged
and adapted translation)

WARM WELCOME, GUEST
**Warm welcome, guest; we ask not who thou art.
If friend thou be, we greet thee with the heart.
If stranger, hands of kindness we extend.
If foe, we will transform thee into friend.**

Welcoming guests into our home (*hachnosas
orchim*) is an important Jewish value. The most
common expression of *hachnosas orchim* is
having guests at our Shabbat table, but it also
includes giving visitors to your city a place to stay.
Wherever Jewish people travel around the world,
they can almost always find a bed and a warm
meal with "family."

*So great is having guests, that it's even greater
than greeting G-d Himself. This we learn from
Abraham that he left G-d in the middle of a
conversation to greet his guests.*
- Talmud, Shabbos 127a

"Rebbi [Yehuda HaNasi] would say: Which is
the right path for man to choose for himself?

Whatever is harmonious *for the one who does it and harmonious for mankind."*
- Ethics of the Fathers 2:1

"Rabbi Eliezer would say: The honor of your fellow should be as precious to you as your own..."
- Ethics of the Fathers 2:10

"Rabbi Akiva, one of the greatest individuals in the Talmud said that the mitzvah of "love your fellow as yourself" is the main principle of the Torah."
- Jerusalem Talmud, Tractate Nedarim 9:4

"A heathen... came to Hillel, and asked him teach him the entire Torah while standing on one foot, Hillel answered, "What is hateful to you, do not do to your neighbor: that is the whole Torah. The rest is commentary; go and learn it."
- Talmud, Tractate Shabbos, 31a

CALL ON ME
If I can help you when in need
Or weary from your labor
Please call on me when in distress
For I'm your friendly neighbor.

OPEN YOUR HAND
Of this known fact
Here is the gist
You can't shake hands
With a tight clenched fist.

"You shall neither take revenge from nor bear a grudge against the members of your people; you shall love your neighbor as yourself. I am the Lord."
- Leviticus 19:18

GIVE 'N LIVE
A life of giving
Makes life worth living.

KINDNESS
Act with kindness as you should
But expect no gratitude.

KINDNESS
Kindness is one thing you can't give away.
It always returns to you doubled someday.

HARVEST
Sow a bit of kindness
Daily, never stop.
Soon friends you'll be reaping.
What a copious crop!

YOUR FAIR SHARE
Happiness I tried to buy
I could not meet the price
For all the treasure of the world
To pay would not suffice.
But happiness has come my way
And I have won it free
By giving to my fellow men
A little bit of me.

Traditional Jewish communities around the world are known for providing informal social services to one another. Neighbor to neighbor services include Free Loan Societies which lend money without interest and free lending programs for household items, medical supplies, clothing and the like. There is a related commandment in Judaism to love other Jews (*ahavas Yisrael*) and to do favors for them, even those with whom we disagree, with whom we are angry or from whom we can never expect repayment. Jewish law requires us to help even an enemy who is in serious trouble or lend objects to an unfriendly neighbor.

"A good neighbor is better than a distant brother."
- Proverbs 27:10

"Woe is to the wicked, woe is to his neighbor, goodness to the righteous, goodness his neighbor."
- Talmud, Tractate Sukkah 56b

"The Alter Rebbe used to say that when you help a friend and take away from your time, it's not really a loss, you will make up the time a thousand fold."
- Or HaTorah B'reishis, Vol. 6 p. 1026b

The Baal Shem Tov would say: *"We cannot imagine how awesome the effects of loving a friend are. When one prays for his friend arousing mercy in Heaven for him, he can annul a bad decree that would have lasted for even seventy*

years and he can turn a curse into a blessing and death into life."
- History of the Previous Lubavitcher Rebbe, Vol. 1, p. 131

"Kindness we do with the dead body (proper burial etc.) is "true kindness" because one does not expect a reward."
- Rashi on Vayechi 47:29

"The Alter Rebbe told his son the Mitteler Rebbe: "Grandfather (the Baal Shem Tov) said that one must have mesiras nefesh (total self-sacrifice and dedication) for ahavas Yisrael (love of one's fellow), even towards a Jew whom one has never seen."
- Hayom Yom, 15 Kislev

SOW SOME COURTESY
Friendships you'll reap
To the greatest degree
When you spend your whole life
Sowing courtesy.

FRUIT BEARING
The kindly word
You speak today
May bear its fruit
Next March or May.

ONE KIND WORD
The sweetest music ever heard
Is made when voicing one kind word.

OPEN INSIDE
As you go through the years
You'll find after you've tried
You can open a pal's heart
Only from the inside.

IT'S ABOUT FACE
When you show a happy face
You enrich the human race.

SMILES
A simple smile – mayhap you know
What power lies therein.
What weight for good . . . . what blessings flow.
What rich rewards smiles win!

Warm friendliness they generate,
Enriching the receiver.
Deep mutual joy kind smiles create,
While naught they cost the giver.

Sweet smiles to many homes have lent
A sprightly mirthful spirit.
Oh, would they were less sparsely spent
When laden with such merit!

In trading, too, smiles play their part.
Good will they build and foster.
Try smiling when you're in the mart –
Smiles never lose their luster.

An antidote for troubled mind,
Bright sunshine to the tired,

A blessing to all humankind –
Their magic power's inspired.

Whene'er you meet along life's way
Souls lonely, sad, and tearful,
With each one leave a laugh that's gay,
Refreshing, lively, cheerful.

And when before the Great White Throne
You stand your God to face,
The joy your smiles have spread is known
Through them you've won His grace.

Kindness and decency (*derech eretz*) is such a value in Judaism that Judaism contributed the Yiddish word *mentsch* (a decent, polite person) to the English language. Two important expressions of *derech eretz* are the ability to greet everyone with a smile and to speak to others with kindness.

"The root of this obligation lies in our obligation toward a human being by virtue of his being a human being."
- Michtav Me'Eliyahu, - Rabbi Eliyahu Dessler, Vol. 4, p. 246

"Words that come from the heart enter the heart of the listener."
- Sefer HaYoshor L'Rabeinu Tam - Rabbi Yaakov ben Meir 1100-1171, Sha'ar 13

"Shammai said, make your Torah study fixed, say little and do much, and receive everyone with a cheerful countenance."
-Ethics of the Fathers, 1:15

The Rebbe once spoke about smiling and he jokingly said, *"In America the custom is that everyone smiles when they greet someone. The law is (Medrash Sh'mos Rabba 47:5) that when you come to a place you need to observe its customs, so we must abide by this custom."*
- <u>Sichos Kodesh</u>, 5741 second day of Rosh Chodesh Av - from a talk of the Lubavitcher Rebbe

IMMORTALITY
It's what you do for others
Most men will agree
Is the virtue that brings
Immortality.

"The Holy Temple (in Jerusalem) was destroyed because of causeless hatred; it will be rebuilt by causeless love."
- Talmud Tractate Yuma 9b (as explained in Likkutei Sichos, Vol. 2 p. 598)

THE RIGHT SPREAD
FOR YOUR BREAD
One cannot live on bread alone
So goes the sage advice,
For one must spread good will and love
To enter paradise.

REWARD
Kindness can't be giv'n away;
It keeps coming back each day.

FOR GETTING OR FOR GIVING?
To enjoy life much more
For a happier living
Be less "for getting"
And more "for giving."

A Jewish person can derive spiritual benefit from acts of kindness (*g'milus chasadim)* in this world and yet still retain spiritual benefit in the next world for the same acts. There is a teaching that acts of kindness are even greater than charity because, while charity can be done only for the poor, acts of kindness can be done both for the rich and for the poor. *"Charity can only benefit the living, but acts of kindness can also be done for the benefit of the deceased."*
- Talmud Tractate Sukkah, 49b

"Love your neighbor as yourself."
According to Rabbi Akiva, this is the main command of the Torah.
- Jerusalem Talmud, Tractate Nedarim, 30b on Leviticus 19:18

If one loves his neighbor he will come to keep all of the commandments of the Torah. Those commandments that are between man and man (not stealing, jealousy, charity, etc.) he will obviously keep [because of his new found love for

all mankind]. And even those between man and G-d (eating kosher, keeping Shabbos, prayer, etc.) he will come to keep because through learning how to love your neighbor you learn to love God.
- Rashi on Tractate Shabbos, 31a

The Alter Rebbe received the following teaching from the Tzaddik Reb Mordechai, who heard it from the Baal Shem Tov: *A soul may descend to this world and live seventy or eighty years in order to do a Jew a material favor, and certainly a spiritual one.*
- Hayom Yom, 5 Iyar

"If one helps his friend God, enlightens both of them."
- Proverbs 29:13 (as understood by the Talmud Tractate Temurah, 16a

MAY I?
If you are silent when a word might bruise,
If you are deaf when gossip is the news,
If you have sympathy for woes of others,
If you believe all humans are your brothers,
If you're courageous when misfortune falls.
If you're alert to answer duties' calls.
Then I say you're a man, men should commend,
And if I find you, may I call you "friend?"

Here, Ellis alludes to two specific Jewish commandments that help shape an individual into a person worthy of admiration – the prohibitions against hurting others with our words (*ona'as devarim*) and against speaking gossip (*lashon hara*). It says, whoever speaks ill of another harms at least three people. The person who is speaking, the one who is the subject of the comment, and the person who is hearing the evil report.

Lashon hara literally means *bad tongue or talk. This means that it is forbidden to speak negatively about someone else, even if it is true.*
- Shulchan Aruch HaRav, Orach Chayim 156:10

Even if one has already heard the lashon hara, it is forbidden to believe it. On the contrary, one should always judge one's fellow favorably.
- Talmud Tractate Pesachim, 118a

Anyone who promotes or maintains disharmony transgresses a Torah prohibition.
- Talmud Tractate Sanhedrin, 110a

CHAPTER 7

BREAK THROUGH WITH JOY

FILL'ER UP WITH HIGH TEST

Life itself can't give you joy
Unless you really will it.
Life just gives you time and space
It's up to you to fill it.

Chapter 7

BREAK THROUGH WITH JOY

"Ivdu es Hashem b'simcha, bo l'fanav bir'nana...
Serve God with gladness; come before Him with songs of joy."
Psalms 100:2

CLOVER ALL OVER
Whenever you're smiling
You're really in clover
And when you are laughing
You feel good all over.

KING FOR A CHEER
When I awake
I always sing
Because the cheerful
Man is king.

HAPPINESS IS THE BEST POLICY
I believe in this song
"A light heart lives long."

"Serve G-d with gladness; come before Him with songs of joy."
Psalms 100:2

The Rambam writes, "The happiness a person should rejoice with when fulfilling mitzvos and having love of G-d is a great service (avoda). There is no greatness or honor other than celebrating before Hashem." The Lubavitcher Rebbe explains that since a Jew is constantly serving Hashem in all he does" he should always be joyful.

"It is a great deed to be joyous at all times!"
-Rabbi Nachman of Breslov

NO ROOM FOR SADNESS
No home is large enough
From the basement to the rafter
If it doesn't have room enough
For plenty of laughter.

WHERE THERE'S LIFE THERE'S HOPE
So long as you're an enthusiast
Just as long will your youth last.

FILL'ER UP WITH HIGH TEST
Life itself can't give you joy
Unless you really will it.
Life just gives you time and space
It's up to you to fill it.

MAKE UP YOUR MIND
Most men are as happy,
To that degree,
That they make up their minds
They are going to be.

It has been revealed to us that the true way of worship is to worship G-d with joy. All thoughts that interfere with this way of worship, thoughts that bring sadness and bitter remorse, especially when magnified by imagination and constant self-appraisal - all such thoughts must be dismissed, for far from helping, they hinder in true worship.
- Excerpt from a letter from the Lubavitcher Rebbe to an individual on the 25th of Tammuz, 5714 July 26, 1954

LIVING LIFE TO THE MAX
Enjoy life and take it
Deliriously
It's too serious to be taken
Seriously.

THE CHASE
Trouble meets you as it's brewed;
Happiness must be pursued.

HAPPINESS
It is not just a station, at which you arrive
But a manner of travelling while you're alive.

King David, in his songs of prayer and praise, writes, "Serve G-d with joy." It is not only the

service in prayer that must be joyful, but all of our activities.
- The Lubavitcher Rebbe, Farbrengen, 10 Shevat, 5742

"You should greet each person with a happy countenance"
-Ethics of the Fathers, 1:15

"Receive every human being with gladness."
Ethics of the Fathers, 3:16

The good-hearted is festive always.
-Proverbs 15:15

A Chasid once wrote to the third Chabad Rebbe, the "Tzemach Tzedek," that he found it difficult to be happy. The Tzemach Tzedek advised him: "Thought, speech and action are within one's control. A person must guard his thoughts and think only thoughts that bring joy; he should be cautious not to speak about sad or depressing matters; and he should behave as if he were very joyous, even if he doesn't feel especially happy. In the end, he will ultimately be joyous."

Clear your mind so that you are not thinking too many thoughts. Your only thought should be: "How do I serve God with joy?" The word b'simcha [with joy] has the same Hebrew letters as the wore machshava [thought]. Therefore, all thoughts that come your way should be directed to serving God joyfully.

- Rabbi Menachem Nachum of Chernobyl

Through these poems, Ellis is highlighting the value of living with joy, no matter what. For, if all is from G-d and for G-d, and everything He does is good, then joy breaks through any apparent concealment and connects us to the good for it to be revealed in this world. Ellis conveys optimism throughout his poetry and though his tone is light and playful, his writings reveal the outlook of our holy Chassidic masters who brought messages of positivity and joy to the masses for generations. Ellis clearly understood that the teaching of our sages; happiness is a choice and it is also a mitzvah. How can we be commanded to be happy? Because when we trust in God wholeheartedly, and believe that all He does is for the good, we can let go of worry and experience true joy in knowing that we are not alone and that we are being cared for at all times.

APPENDIX

Books By Michael F. Ellis

Rhymes Without Reason

Rhyme Doesn't Pay

Ellis in Wonderland

Prhyme Ribs

Rhyme on the Rocks

Rhyme-atic Fever

Rhyme Marches On

Having a Wonderful Rhyme

A Rhyme A Dozen

In the Rhyme-Light

Once Upon A Rhyme

It's Just About Rhyme

Not Required Reading

A Book of Rare Poems

Books by Michael F. Ellis

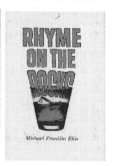

Books by Michael F. Ellis

Books by Michael F. Ellis

WHO'S WHO

Ellis, Michael Franklin, partner Ellis Advertising Company, Statler Hilton Hotel, Buffalo, N.Y. 14202. Partner Ellis Public Relations Co.

Areas of exp.: acct. supvn., creative dir., media; banking svces, political campaigns, beer, Mem: Niagara Frontier Trans. Auth. p.r. consultant, Buffalo Better Bus. Bur., C. of C., Boost Buffalo Assn., Greater Buffalo Adv. Club (past dir.), Epilepsy Assn. of Western N.Y. bd. mem. (past pres.), Deaconess Hospital bd. mem., Small Bus. Adm.-Western N.Y. founder & adv. bd. mem. Service Corps of Retired Execs. advisory bd., moo Plus Club (past section chmn.), Nat'l Conf. Christian & Jews, Beta Sigma Rho Fndtn. advisory bd., Ancient Landmark's Lodge, Buffalo Consistory, Ismailia Temple (Shrine), United Comml. Travelers, Union of Amer. Hebrew Congs., Erie Cty. Past Masters Ass'n, Beta Sigma Rho (past nat'l pres.), Good Fellows, W. N.Y. Geriatrics So., Buffalo Auto Club, Hospital permanent mem., Montefiore Club, Variety Club, Ontario Turf Club, 33rd Degree Masonic Club W. N.Y., B'nai B'rith, Temple Beth Zion; former Finl. Public Relations Assoc., Mayor's Comm. on War Time Recreation v-chmn., Selective Svce. Appeal Bd. W. N.Y. chmn., B'nai B'rith Dist. 1 mem. bd. GOVs., Jewish Fed. for Social Svce. dir., Salvation Army, Protestant Home for Unprotected Children, Muscular Dystrophy Fund Chmn., Erie Cty. Boy Scouts, Ellicott Eye Clinic Children's Hospital pres., Emergency Hospital advisory bd. mem.,

WHO'S WHO

Philharmonic Orch., Easter Seal Campaign chmn. W. N.Y., Villa Maria Coll. bd. mem., Buffalo Zoological Soc. bd. mem., Sisters of Charity Hospital fund dir. p.r., Temple Beth Zion trustee, Hutchinson-Central H.S. Alum. Ass'n pres., Educ: U. of Buffalo, Fillmore Coll. Auth: *Rhymes Without Reason* 1962, *Rhyme Doesn't Pay* 1963, *Ellis in Wonderland* 1964, *Prhyme, Ribs* 1962, *Rhyme on the Rocks* 1966, *Rhyme-Atic Fever* 1967, *Rhyme Marches On* 1968, *Having a Wonderful Rhyme* 1969, *A Rhyme a Dozen* 1970. Rec: 33rd Degree Masonic Jewel, Pres. Truman Medal for Selective Service Appeal Bd., Printers' Ink adv. & p.r. medal, Masonic Meritorious Svce. Plaque & Jewel, Beta Sigma Rho Man of the Year Award, City of Buffalo Good Neighbor's Award, Emil Rubenstein Humanitarian Award, Epilepsy Assn. citation & plaque, Muscular Dystrophy Ass'n citation & plaque.

Born Jun. 11, 1896 Buffalo, N.Y.; m. Corinne F. Eloskey Feb. 12, 1920; ch. Michael F. Jr., Dr. Robert Ellis (dec.), Joan (Mrs. Samuel Shatkin), Jewish. Home: Delaware Towers, 1088 Delaware Ave., Buffalo, N.Y. 14209.

About the Author

It is said that Michael F. Ellis has a secret source of supply for the hours he needs each day to accomplish all that his busy calendar demands. And it would certainly seem so when you see the long and impressive list of organizations in which he takes an active part without neglecting his responsibilities as an advertising executive, family man and poet.

Mr. Ellis is a member of hospital boards and health foundations; he serves on multitudinous civic, state and national committees. He is on the advisory board of banks and colleges; participates enthusiastically in fraternal affairs. He is a fund raiser and community idea man; gives freely. of his time to religious and interfaith causes, and works wholeheartedly for the elderly.

His citations cover the walls of his office and his many honors include recognition for meritorious deeds too numerous to mention. His way of life is best described by the statement, "When you want something done and done well, ask the busiest man you know to do it." It's usually Mike Ellis.

Dear Michael,   Jan. 15, 1981

We all enjoyed the article about you in Downtown but then we all respect you and what you stand for every day.

Please accept our heartfelt applause.

Sincerely,

Betty Ryan Mahoney
Spce Assistant, Bob Zugger

CITY OF BUFFALO
OFFICE OF THE MAYOR

JAMES D. GRIFFIN
MAYOR

December 15, 1980

Mr. Michael Ellis
Ellis Advertising
Statler Hilton Hotel
Buffalo, N.Y. 14202

Dear Mr. Ellis:

Thank you for your delightful book, "Once Upon A Rhyme."

Your thoughtfulness is much appreciated. Best wishes to you for a very happy holiday season.

Sincerely,

James D. Griffin

JDG/cs

THE WHITE HOUSE
WASHINGTON

April 17, 1975

Dear Brother Ellis:

It is always a special pleasure to hear from a fellow Mason, and I am particularly delighted to have your note. April 10, I was deeply honored to receive the Georgian Medal and will treasure it forever. Thank you so much for your thoughtfulness in writing.

Fraternally yours,

Gerald R. Ford

Mr. Michael F. Ellis
Chairman of the Board
Ellis Advertising Company
The Statler Hilton
Niagara Square
Buffalo, New York 14202

THE WHITE HOUSE
WASHINGTON

September 17, 1974

PERSONAL

Dear Mr. Ellis:

Thank you for the inscribed copy of your book of poems. I deeply appreciate your thoughtfulness and what you to know how grateful I am for your expression of goodwill. Having the support and prayers of fine people like you is indeed a source of strength and encouragement to me.

My family and I join in sending you warm best wishes.

Sincerely,

Gerald R. Ford

Mr. Michael F. Ellis
The Statler Hilton
Niagara Square
Buffalo, New York 14202

ALWAYS USE ZIP

THE WHITE HOUSE

Mr. Michael F. Ellis
Chairman of the Board
Ellis Advertising Company
The Statler Hilton

Various Dedications from Gramp's Books

This, my 12th book, *IT'S JUST ABOUT RHYME*, I am happy to dedicate to my dear mother, Rhoda Brown Ellis, now long deceased. It was on her lap and in her arms that I was first exposed to the enjoyment of rhymes and jingles. I can still remember excerpts from some, like "The maiden all forlorn who milked the cow with a crumpled horn," "There was a crooked man who walked a crooked mile," and countless others. My mother, born in Buffalo, was a very proper mid-victorian lady who throughout her entire life called legs, "limbs," and clothing "inner garments and outer garments." She always dressed in black with a little black hat perched on top of her head and in her entire life never used a slang expression or said an uncomplimentary word about anyone.

I am sure God is watching over her beautiful soul.

This book I dedicate to my daughter Joan (Mrs. Samuel Shatkin) whose creativity and involvement in civic, philanthropic and family life have been a source of great pleasure and pride to me throughout the years.

This book I dedicate to my dear wife, CORINNE, my manager, superintendent, help-mate, secretary, nurse, purchasing agent, cook, chairman-of-thehouse, servant, and boss for 47 years.

This book is written in honor of my 87th birthday. On Lincoln's Birthday, my wife, Corrine F. Ellis and I were married 65 years. I still attend business every day and I am in the office from 9am to 4pm daily. The Ellis Advertising Co. was founded by me in 1924 and is now 60 years old.

APPRECIATION

In appreciation, the author is pleased to acknowledge the cooperation of Beatrice Haniford, Shirley Massey, Barbara Hale and Thomas Moore, members of the staff of the Ellis Advertising, Public Relations & Research Company, who gave of their time to help bring this volume of verse to fruition. Special thanks are also due Hoffman Printers for typography and the Niagara Photo Engraving Company for engraving.
MICHAEL F. ELLIS

A Word of Thanks for Assistance on Gramp's Last Volume:

A Book of Rare Poems
(Rare Because They're Not Well Done)

I proffer my heartfelt thanks to Darcy F. Shatkin for the painstaking help given me in compiling these versifications for publication.

INSCRIPTION:

Personal Book Inscriptions from Gramp to
Nana, Mom and Darcy

nov 24, 1983

To my wife, Corinne
all my love,
Mike

To my sweet daughter
Joan
my "Who's Who"
Love
Dad

To my dear grand-daughter,
Darcy, the curley-headed
giggler — the deep-thinker
who always says "Well"
Love
Gramp
Dec 18/63

INSCRIPTION:

Personal Book Inscriptions from Gramp to Darcy

> To my granddaughter, Darcy
> A darling girl,
> who will surely
> grow-up to be———
> "the world's finest
> telephone operator"———
> Love
> Gramp
>
> Dec 25/63

> To my singing little girl,
> Darcy
> Love
> Gramp

> To my "Darcy Dear"
> Love
> Gramp
>
> Dec 25/68

My Legacy from Gramp

ASSIGNMENT

FOR VALUE RECEIVED, the receipt and sufficiency of which are hereby acknowledged, the undersigned, MICHAEL F. ELLIS, SR. ("Ellis") hereby grants, assigns and delivers to DARCY F. SHATKIN ("Shatkin") the right to set to music any and all of the original works of poetry composed by Ellis, whether now or hereafter existing and whether published by Ellis or in manuscript form (such works, as set to music, are hereinafter called the "composed works") and in connection therewith: (i) the right to record, dulpicate, print, publish, sell and distribute copies of the composed works, (ii) the right to public performance of the composed works, whether on radio, television, stage, screen or any other similar or different medium, (iii) the right to grant licenses of all types and of every nature with respect to the composed works, (iv) the right to obtain a copyright to any and all of the composed works, (v) the right to make or have made adaptations, arrangements, interpretations, additions, subtractions and/or changes in and to the composed works, and (vi) the absolute and unqualified right to use the composed works in any manner or form deemed reasonable by Shatkin; provided, however, that Shatkin shall acknowledge and credit Ellis, when reasonably possible in the circumstances, but only when reasonably appropriate in light of Ellis' standing and reputation in the community as of this date, as a source of such works.

IN WITNESS WHEREOF, the undersigned has executed this Assignment this _16ᵗʰ_ day of August, 1982.

Michael F. Ellis
Michael F. Ellis, Sr.

Glossary of Terms

Adon Olam – "Master of the World;" one of the most well-known hymns in the Jewish prayer book. According to tradition, it was composed in the 11th century by the great spiritual poet, Solomon ibn Gabirol. The lyrics of this hymn speak about God's greatness and all-enlivening existence. "Master of the world, Who reigned before everything as created, at the time when by His will all things were made, then was His name proclaimed King, and after all things shall cease to be, the Awesome One Will reign alone…"

Ahavat Yisrael – The Torah (Vayikra-Leviticus, 19:18) enjoins every Jew to "love your fellow as yourself," which Rashi, the Torah's foremost commentator, describes as being, "a great principle of the Torah – according to Rabbi Akiva." The Alter Rebbe explains that every Jew's real essence is his Godly soul, and despite everyone's differences, they all stem from the same Godly source. Thus, the commandment to love a fellow Jew is a directive to go beyond the physical, to focus on another Jew's essence and see it as it truly is – with one's own essence.

The Arizal – Rabbi Isaac HaLevi Luria (1534-1572); the famed master Kabbalist who lived in (Tsfat) Safed and shared with his students a new approach in Kabbalah – Lurianic Kabbalah – which serves as the basis for most of the subsequent works of Kabbalah.

Atzlut – Sluggishness, idleness, or laziness. According to Chassidic teachings, this attribute derives from the spiritual element of earth. Each of the four elements (i.e., Air, Fire, Earth, Water) relate to different aspects of one's natural traits. Atzlut is an expression of the animal soul's element of earth: just as the earth is characterized by heaviness, so, too, does one with atzlut experience a heaviness of the body, along with feelings of depression and sadness.

Avodah – "service," "work," or "effort;" the labor invested in one's service of God via learning Torah and performing Mitzvot. Such efforts are necessary in order to overcome one's nature, habits, and the opposing drives of their animalistic nature. The word is related to the concept of "ibud orot" (tanning hides) – i.e., avodah refines and changes one's nature like the tanning process alters the nature of the leather. In Chabad Chassidic terminology, avodah often refers to prolonged prayer (avodat hatefillah) that includes meditation on Godly concepts. This helps a person internalize their learning, translate it into deeply-felt inspiration, and refine their character traits.

The Baal Shem Tov – Literally, "Master of the good name;" the founder of the Chassidic movement, Rabbi Yisrael (ben Eliezer) Baal Shem Tov was born in Ukraine in 1698 on the 18th day of Elul. His father, Rabbi Eliezer, was a member of the secret circle of righteous tzaddikim. He passed away when Yisrael was only five, empowering his son with his final words: "Fear nothing but Hashem, and love every Jew with all your heart and all your soul." Orphaned Yisrael wandered the forests for years in meditation and maintained simple jobs to disguise his developing greatness and identity. He grew and attained the level where he was accepted to the same circle of tzaddikim. On his 36th birthday, it was revealed to him that the time had come to publicly disseminate his teachings on the inner dimension of Torah – Pnimiyut HaTorah. His teachings emphasize that every creation contains a spark of Godliness; that God has tremendous love for each and every one of His children, scholar and simple Jew alike; and the importance of joy and simple faith in serving Hashem, rather than asceticism. Although he initially encountered fierce opposition from the scholarly elite, many later became his devoted disciples. He passed away at the age of 62 on Shavuot in 1760, and was succeeded by his main student, Rabbi DovBer of Mezeritch (1700-1772).

Bitachon – Trust in God, versus faith ("emunah") where one believes that God can change any situation for the better. Bitachon implies a certainty that things not only can, but will get better and that goodness will prevail, even for the undeserving. Thus, bitachon is an active, lifelong effort. As phrased by the Previous Rebbe (Rebbe Rayatz), Rabbi Yosef Yitzchok Schneerson (1880–1950): "Bitachon is more than hope. A person who has bitachon believes that what he hoped for will certainly eventuate. In fact, it is already present. The obstacle exists only in the person himself."

Bereishit – Genesis; the first book of the 5 books of the Torah (Bible): Shemot (Exodus), Vayikra (Leviticus), Bamidbar (Numbers), Devarim (Deuteronomy). Bereishit starts with the story of the world's creation and the descent of mankind from Adam and Eve. It includes the lives of the Patriarchs (Abraham, Isaac, and Jacob), Matriarchs (Sarah, Rebekah, Leah, and Rachel), and the 12 Tribes. God promises the land of Israel to the Patriarchs. However, they will endure slavery before it is realized. And, thus, the book ends with Jacob and all his family descending to Egypt to meet up with Joseph and escape the regional famine.

Bitul Z'man – "wasting time;" there is a constant obligation to use our time in Torah study, fulfillment of commandments, or other meaningful and purposeful activities.

Chabad – an acronym for Chochmah, Binah, and Da'at: the three intellectual powers of the soul (wisdom, understanding, and knowledge). As a movement, the name speaks to its system of Jewish religious philosophy: the deepest dimension of Hashem's Torah, which teaches understanding and recognition of the Creator, the role and purpose of creation, and the importance and unique mission of each creature. This approach to serving Hashem and living a Godly life, guides a person to refine and govern his every act and feeling through wisdom, comprehension and knowledge.

Chassidic, Chassidut – a revolutionary approach to Judaism that emphasizes the unique preciousness of every soul, a personal relationship with God, and joy in performing commandments and learning Torah. The Chassidic movement within Judaism was founded by the Baal Shem Tov. His goals was to awaken the Jewish People to their innermost essence by way of the Torah's innermost dimension, and thereby prepare the world for redemption and ultimate perfection. Its teachings represents the greatest expansion and development of the Torah's inner dimension and the teachings of Kabbalah – rendering graspable the deepest mysteries of the universe, both of the God and the soul, and inspiring a Jew's relationship with his Creator.

Derech Eretz – literally, "the way of the land;" how people tend to act or how they should act. In common usage, it means acting with kindness and respect, particularly towards parents, elders, and teachers.

Elijah (Eliyahu) – famous prophet with whom the announcement of the future redemption is closely linked. According to Torah tradition, he often descends to earth to help Jews in distress or reveal Torah secrets to great scholars. He is present at every brit milah ceremony and visits every Passover seder. He is famous for successfully challenging the prophets of Ba'al at Mt. Carmel. Tradition teaches that Eliyahu did not die, rather ascended to heaven alive in a fiery chariot in 718 BCE. He was succeeded by his student Elisha.

Eishet Chayil – literally, "A Woman of Valor;" 22-verse hymn found in the closing verses of Mishlei. Traditionally sung in Jewish homes on Friday night prior to the Shabbat meal, the prayer extols the praises of the woman of the house. On a deeper, kabbalistic level, the song is a greeting for the Divine presence that is manifest on Shabbat.

Emunah – faith, which is part of a Jew's essential connection to Hashem, resulting from the fact that his soul is an actual part of God. The uniquely Jewish, God-linked soul, and the emunah it generates, is an inheritance to every Jew from the patriarchs and matriarchs; particularly from Abraham, the "first believer." As such, it is always present, though not necessarily conscious. Emunah finds expression in a Jew's innate readiness to devote himself to the service of Hashem and sacrifice his life for His sake. Emunah is also related to the word "imun", meaning "practice" or "training." Revealing one's inherent awareness of, and sensitivity to Hashem, requires practice and training. Moreover, it is the function of the soul of Moses – present in every generation's Torah leaders – to sustain and reinforce Jewish faith.

Farbrengen – Yiddish, "gathering;" Chassidic gatherings convened in honor of special dates, communal or personal events, holidays, and other occasions. Usually led by a rabbi or spiritual guide (mashpia), farbrengens offer participants an opportunity to receive encouragement and express their soul struggles. In between the singing of Chassidic niggunim (typically wordless, soulful melodies) and toasting "l'chaim" (literally, 'to life'), those present share insights, practical ideas, and stories that inspire each other to grow and improve. The experience is an actualization of a teaching from the Mitteler Rebbe, the second Lubavitcher Rebbe – Rabbi Dovber Schneerson (1773–1827): "When two Jews meet, and one tells the other what ails his heart, the result is two Godly Souls taking on a single Animal Soul."

In addition, the Lubavitcher Rebbe (as well as his predecessors) frequently hosted large farbrengens, which served as his primary medium of teaching. They each lasted several hours, consisting of long talks (sichot) on the week's Torah reading and significant upcoming events on the Jewish calendar, as well as profound mystical discourses (ma'amarim) explaining passages from the Talmud, Kabbalah, or Chassidic teachings. Between the Rebbe's words, the thousands in attendance sang niggunim and raised small cups of wine to toast "l'chaim" to the Rebbe.

Gilgulim – "cycles," "recycling," or "reincarnations;" the return of the soul to a physical body in the world for the purposes of rectifying an issue in a previous life or accomplish something that was not accomplished in a previous life.

G'milut Chasadim – "acts of kindness;" a Torah-virtue comprised of personal acts of kindness: charity, visiting the sick, hospitality, burying the dead, funding weddings of poor brides and grooms, extending interest-free loans, and comforting mourners, among others. The Mishnah teaches (Pirkei Avot 1:2): "The world stands on three things: Torah, Divine service, and gemilut chassadim." Elsewhere in the Mishnah (Pe'ah 1:1), gemilut chassadim is listed among the things for which no limit has been prescribed by the Torah, as well as providing immediate benefit besides ultimate reward later in heaven.

Hachnasat Orchim – "welcoming guests;" the important Jewish value of hospitality, providing for visitors and guests in one's home.

Hashem – literally,, "the Name;" referring to the "ineffable name of God," treating God's name with reverence is a way to give Him respect. As such, it is common Jewish practice to restrict the use of the names of God to prayer so as keep His "name Holy," Various names of God are given subtle permutations (i.e., Havaya [Yud-Hey-Vav-Hey], Elokim, Ado-nai, E-l, etc.) In casual conversation, God is often referred to as "Hashem."

Hakarat Hatov – "acknowledging good;" having gratitude and appreciation of the good God bestows upon us, recognizing the kindnesses others do for us. Recognizing the blessings in life and seeing things in a "positive" light.

Hayom Yom - the Lubavitcher Rebbe's (Rabbi Menachem Mendel Schneerson's) first book, compiled in 1942 upon the request of the Rebbe Rayatz (Rabbi Yosef Yitzchok Shneerson). HaYom Yom is a compilation of Chasidic sayings, teachings, ideas, and customs, arranged according to the days of the year. It has become a treasured Chassidic work that is learned daily for inspiration and guidance.

Ibn Pakuda – 11th century sage and writer on Jewish thought (1040-1080); his most acclaimed work is Chovot Halevavot (Duties of the Heart), which methodically details and outlines a person's Divine service. Such theme included in this rich

Kabbalah, Kabbalistic – literally, receiving [the tradition]; the Torah's esoteric, mystical dimension. Also called "soul" of the Torah, it is the deepest level of Torah explanation and comprehension. Kabbalah views Torah and life from the perspective of the underlying spiritual reality that births everything in the universe. Endeavoring to understand these forces and their effects grants one insight into the essential unity within creation, and thereby fulfill the precept, "Know the God of your father." Kabbalah and its teachings are an integral part of the Torah and included in the collective wisdom and instruction that God gave the Jews at Mount Sinai. In the 2nd century C.E., Rabbi Shimon bar Yochai (Rashbi) committed this knowledge to paper for the first time, authoring the Zohar. The Arizal, Tsfat mystic Rabbi Yitzchak Luria (1534-1572 CE), pioneered Kabbalah's expansion into the modern era with "Lurianic Kabbalah," famously proclaiming that the time had come for wider revelation of mystical teachings. The Chassidic movement, founded by the Baal Shem Tov (1698-1760), and the revelation of the teachings of Chassidut marked the third wave of expansion for this innermost dimension of Torah (Pnimiyut HaTorah); a necessity in order to revive the "fainting" souls of the Jewish people while in exile, and to help prepare for redemption.

Lashon Hara – literally, "evil tongue;" the Torah prohibition against speaking negatively of another person even if it's true. Moreover, not only is it forbidden to speak it, it's also forbidden to listen to it.

L'chatchila Ariber – "to begin with, go over it;" phrase coined by the Rebbe Maharash, the fourth Lubavitcher Rebbe, which embodies his approach to dealing with challenges and difficulties in life. "The world says: 'If you can't go under, leap over; I say: In the first place, go over!'" With this aphorism, he encouraged his Chassidim to always tackle an obstacle head on and transcend above it.

Lubavitcher; a Lubavitch Chassid – a pious follower of the Lubavitcher Rebbe and adherent of the teachings of Chabad-Lubavitch Chassidism.

The Lubavitcher Rebbe, Rabbi Menachem M. Schneerson – (April 5, 1902-June 12, 1994), known to many as "the Rebbe," was an Orthodox rabbi, and the seventh and last Lubavitcher Rebbe. He is considered one of the most influential Jewish leaders of the 20th century. An acknowledged Torah genius from early childhood, he married the sixth Rebbe's (Rayatz) daughter, Rebbetzin Chaya Mushka in Warsaw in 1929. Later he engaged in advanced studies of mathematics and the sciences in the University of Berlin and then at the Sorbonne in Paris. The couple miraculously arrived in the United States on June 23, 1941, and the Rebbe assumed many leadership positions within the Lubavitch movement, bolstering and disseminating Torah, Judaism, and the teachings and approach to life of Chassidut. He assumed the leadership of Lubavitch a year after his father-in-law's passing in 1950.

Maggid – an itinerant preacher, skilled as a narrator of stories.

Mentsch – Yiddish, literally a "human being;" a person of integrity and honor, an upstanding member of society who leads an ethical life.

Mesirut Nefesh – literally, "giving over the soul" or "self-sacrifice;" the Torah holds preservation of human life paramount and expects a Jew to violate Jewish law in order to save lives. There are, however, three prohibitions that are not to be transgressed under any circumstance and one forfeits his life (if necessary): idolatry, sexual misconduct, and murder. This self-sacrifice is considered an act of sanctifying Hashem's name (Kiddush Hashem). According to the teachings of Chassidut, a Jew's inherent, incomprehensible ability to sacrifice his life rather than convert or openly deny Hashem and Judaism, is proof that he possess a Godly Soul that is inseparably connected to Hashem, and which harbors a powerful, fiery love of Hashem. Mesirut Nefesh can also be applied to one's general observance of Torah and Mitzvot when opposed by government bans, anti-Semitism, or other danger or threat to life.

Mezuzah (pl., Mezuzot) – lit., "doorpost;" parchment scrolls affixed to the doorposts of Jewish homes and businesses. They feature the first two paragraphs of the Shema prayer (Devarim 6:4-9 and 11:13-21), which direct: "And you shall inscribe them upon the doorposts of your house and upon your gates." Written on the back of the parchment is Hashem's name: "Shaddai (shin-dalet-yud)" – ("Almighty"); also interpreted as an acronym for "Shomer Daltot Yisrael" ("Guardian of the doors of the Jewish people"). The scroll is commonly encased for protection and affixed to the right-hand doorpost within the top one-third of the frame. The mezuzah serves as a reminder of Hashem's presence and many are accustomed to touch it and kiss their hand when entering and leaving.

Middot – "traits;" the seven emotional attributes of the soul (subconscious) which produce emotions we feel and express, or a general expression for a person's character traits.

Mikvah – literally, "collection" or "gathering;" collection of "living water" (i.e., rain, springs, or flowing rivers) used for the purpose of ritual immersion and purification. Nowadays, its main uses include: a woman achieving ritual purity after menstruation or childbirth; Jewish men achieving greater purity daily before prayer, or in personal preparation for Shabbat and Yom-Tov (holidays); as part of the conversion procedure; and to render certain utensils ready for use with food. A mikvah must contain enough water to cover the entire body of an average-sized person – at least 40 se'ah of water (approximately 150 gallons), which is supplied by a naturally occurring source, such as rivers, lakes, and springs. A cistern filled by rain may also constitute a mikvah's water supply. As long as the minimum 40 se'ah quantity derives from a natural, live source, the total volume can be topped off with tap water and other unnatural sources.

The Mitteler Rebbe – Rabbi DovBer Schneuri (1773-1827), the second Rebbe of Lubavitch and the son of the Alter Rebbe, the founder of Chabad Chassidut.

Mishlei (Proverbs) – the second book in the Ketuvim (Writings), which is the third section of the TaNaCh: Torah, Nevi'im (Prophets), Ketuvim. It was written by King Solomon and features his wise sayings and parables.

Mishna – the first written compilation of the Oral Law, authored and systematically codified by Rabbi Yehudah HaNasi (approximately 200 C.E.). Generations of discussion and commentary on the Mishnah's laws served as the basis for the Talmud.

Mitzvah – literally, "commandment" related to the word for "connection". These are the 613 God-given commandments of the Torah that are the means of connecting with God. These Mitzvot subdivide into 248 positive Mitzvot and 365 negative Mitzvot (transgressions) corresponding to various limbs and sinews of the body. In its common usage, however, the word connotes all of the laws, practices, and customs that constitute Jewish law and observance. According to Chassidut, the word "Mitzvah" relates to "tzavta" (Aramaic, "attachment"), hinting at the bond it forges between Hashem (the Commander) and man (the commanded).

Mussar – literally, "instruction" or "discipline;" Jewish ethical, educational, and cultural movement that arose in 19th century Eastern Europe, particularly among non-Chassidic, Lithuanian Jews. Its founder, Rabbi Yisrael Lipkin Salanter (1810-1883), used the term "mussar" to refer to the disciplined efforts at ethical and spiritual development, self-perfection, correction, and those religious obligations not fully specified in halachah. The movement began in response to declining traditional Jewish observance caused by the Enlightenment, the corresponding Haskalah movement, and prevailing conditions of anti-Semitism, Jewish assimilation, poverty, and poor living conditions.

Nachat – pride and delightful contentment, typically referring to that which derives from children.

Nachmanides – Rabbi Moshe ben Nachman, also known by the acronym Ramban (1194 – 1270), was a leading medieval Jewish scholar and Rabbinic leader, as well as a philosopher, Kabbalist, and practicing physician, who lived in Spain. His famous works include commentaries on the Torah and the Talmud, and many smaller works of halacha, mussar, and philosophy. He also penned several well-known letters that addressed issues throughout Jewish communities. His famous 1263 defense of Judaism before a panel of Church representatives in Barcelona was so successful that they banned him to exile.

Ob"m – an abbreviation for the honorific "of blessed memory" used when speaking of someone deceased. The abbreviation is found after the name of the deceased on gravestones and memorial walls inside synagogues.

Omer, Sefirat HaOmer – The omer was a measurement of barley that was offered up in the Temple in Jerusalem. "Sefirat HaOmer" ("the Counting of the Omer") is the Mitzvah of formally counting the 49 days from the second day of Pesach until erev (the day before) Shavuot when that offering was made. The counting serves as a preparation for receiving the Torah on Shavuot.

Ona'at Devarim – the Torah prohibition against causing pain or anguish to another with words, based on the verse (Vayikra, 25:17): "Do not aggrieve one another."

Passover – in Hebrew, Pesach. The eight-day festival (seven days in Israel) from the 15th through the 22nd of the Hebrew month of Nissan, which commemorates God's redeeming the Jewish people from their enslavement in ancient Egypt.

Pirkei Avot – literally, Chapters of the Fathers (Ethics of the Fathers); a unique tractate of the Mishna (see Talmud) which that discusses the Torah's views on morals, ethics, values, and interpersonal relationships.

Rabbeinu Bachaye – (1255-1340) famous Spanish philosopher and scholar, best known for his Torah commentary.

Rabbi Dov Ber, the Maggid of Mezritch – the second leader of the Chassidic movement; he succeeded the Baal Shem Tov, strengthening the movement, and solidified its place in Judaism. He was the spiritual mentor of the Alter Rebbe, Rabbi Schneur Zalman of Liadi, who founded the Chabad approach of Chassidut.

Rabbi Nachman of Breslov – (1772-1810), was the founder of the Breslov Chassidic movement and a great-grandson of the Baal Shem Tov. His approach concentrated on closeness to God, going into isolation (hitbodedut), and speaking to God in normal conversation as one would with a friend.

Rabbi Schneur Zalman of Liadi – (1745-1812) commonly referred to as "the Alter Rebbe;" the founder and first Rebbe of Chabad-Lubavitch Chassidut, who famously authored the Chassidic masterpiece, Tanya, and Halacha masterpiece, Shulchan Aruch HaRav. The Chabad system uniquely renders the deepest of Godly concepts within the mind's grasp so that one may contemplate them and generate feelings towards the Creator, which then inspire actions and passion in one's observance.

Rabbi Yehuda HaNasi – also called "Rebbi;" was elected the religious and spiritual leader of the Jewish people after the passing of his father, Rabbi Shimon Ben Gamliel. He is credited with writing the Mishna, the first written compilation of the Oral Law in approximately 200 C.E. Many stories are told of her tremendous personal piety, and his great wealth, which he freely distributed to the poor and needy.

Rambam – Rabbi Moses ben Maimon (1135-1204); one of the foremost writers on Jewish law, his 14 volume Mishneh Torah codified all of Talmudic law and continues to be authoritative. He also achieved fame as a communal leader, preeminent medieval Jewish philosopher, and prolific physician.

Rashi – Rabbi Shlomo Yitzchaki (1040-1105); famous medieval French commentator on the entire TaNaCh (Torah, Nevi'im/Prophets, Ketuvim/Writings) and Talmud. His acclaimed commentaries are widely read to this day and serve as the standard for understanding the basic meaning of the text.

Rebbe - A righteous and pious scholar and leader of a Chassidic sect. The position is typically inherited dynastically, handed from father to son, or close relative. The Rebbe leads, guides, and directs his Chassidim and their community, aiding them in their personal issues, both spiritual and physical.

Rebbe Maharash – Rabbi Shmuel Schneerson (1834-1882), the fourth Lubavitcher Rebbe.

Rebbe Rayatz – Rabbi Yosef Yitzchok Schneerson (1880–1950); the previous Lubavitcher Rebbe, sixth in the Lubavitcher dynasty.

Shabbat – literally, "rest" or "cessation [of work]"); also known as "Shabbos." The divinely-ordained day of rest, sanctification and celebration that begins on Friday at sunset and ends on the following evening after nightfall. The Talmud teaches that it is equivalent to all the other commandments and enumerates 39 forbidden creative acts that one is to refrain from on Shabbat.

Schtick – Yiddish; a gimmick, comic routine, special talent, or style of performance associated with a particular person.

Shavuot – literally, "weeks;" corresponding to the seven weeks between Pesach and Shavuot. One of the three Pilgrimage Festivals (Pesach, Shavuot, and Sukkot), Shavuot commemorates the momentous occasion of God's giving the Torah to the Jewish people on Mount Sinai, and it marks the completion of the seven-weeks of counting that begins on Passover.

Sicha (pl. Sichot) – literally, "talk;" Torah talk delivered by one of the Chabad Rebbeyim discussing a wide range of topics: holidays, weekly Torah portion, personal avodah, prayer, the performance of Mitzvot, challenges of the time, and more.

Talmid Chacham – literally, a "student of wisdom;" title used to refer to a Torah scholar.

Talmud – literally, "learning" (synonymous with Gemara); Talmud is the most crucial work of Torah Shebe'al peh (The Oral Law) and the primary authority for all rulings of Jewish law. It endeavors to capture the spirit of Judaism's oral tradition first received by Moses at Mount Sinai and verbally taught and transmitted from teacher to student throughout the generations. It features the discussions, debates, and stories of the time's greatest scholars in explication of the brief legal summaries found in the Mishnah – the first written codification of The Oral Law. There are two Talmuds: one completed in Israel during the fourth century (Talmud Yerushalmi) and one completed in Babylonia in the fifth century (Talmud Bavli).

Tehillim – Psalms; one of the books of the Writings (TaNaCh): Torah, Nevi'im (Prophets), Ketuvim (Writings). Famously composed by King David, they features praises of God's greatness, goodness, and mercy, and represent the most powerful prayers known to man.

Tikkun – "fixing" or "rectification;" a reference to one working on their own character traits or dealing with the consequences of sin and mistakes made. It also refers to effect of our actions to heal and complete a world intentional created imperfect by God.

Torah – literally, "teaching;" commonly refers to the Five Books of Moses (Bible, Old Testament). Also used more generally to describe the body of Jewish religious teachings encompassing all Jewish law (Talmud, halacha), practice, and tradition.

Tzaddik (pl. Tzaddikim) – "a righteous person;" in the language of our Sages throughout the Talmud, a tzaddik is one whose good deeds exceeds his bad deeds and would be vindicated in judgment. According to the teachings of Chassidut, however, a tzaddik is essentially different from ordinary people, and a level achieved by few. He completely sublimates and transforms his animalistic nature and soul, views anything that contradicts

Hashem's will to be repulsive, and exclusively dedicates his desires, feelings, and thoughts to Hashem. "The life of the tzaddik is not a life of the flesh, but a life of spirituality, [consisting of] his faith in Hashem, his awe of Hashem, and his love of Hashem" (Tanya - Iggeret HaKodesh, Ch. 27).

Tzemach Tzedek – Rabbi Menachem Mendel Schneerson (1789-1866), the third Lubavitcher Rebbe and grandson of the Alter Rebbe, Rabbi Schneur Zalman of Liadi who founded the Chabad movement.

Yahrtzeit – (Yiddish) "a year's time;" the anniversary of someone's passing.

About the Author

MICHAEL FRANKLIN ELLIS

Michael Franklin Ellis was born June 11, 1896 and educated in Buffalo, NY, where he learned and then taught the art of advertising, publicity, public relations, and business administration. He went to Hutchinson Tech High School and then he got his start working under his very own father Newman Ellis, who had a smoking pipe company called The Ellis Pipe House. It was through promoting the company that he got his start in advertising. He soon became a teacher and mentor to many throughout the advertising and public relations industry. He established Ellis Advertising Company in Buffalo in 1924—one of the first advertising companies in Western New York. Because Ellis had a humorous outlook on life, he was able to see the lighter side of every situation, which is captured in his many books of poetry. With book titles like: "Rhymes without Reason, Rhyme Doesn't Pay, Ellis in Wonderland, Prhyme Ribs, Rhyme Marches On, A Rhyme

A Dozen, In The Rhyme-Light," etc., one can definitely gain a sense of Ellis' sense of humor.

Ellis served as either an officer or on the board of over 20 community and civic institutions, and participated in dozens more clubs and organizations. That was Mike Ellis. To know Mike was to know a devoted husband and family man, a sports enthusiast, a poet, a comedian, a clever businessman, and community leader. One of the secrets to his success he attributed to his wife, Corinne (Eloskey) Ellis. She was his inspiration for life and work. Michael and Corinne had three children, who blessed them with eleven grandchildren, twenty-two great-grandchildren and four great-great grandchildren and counting!

Michael F. Ellis seemed to have a secret supply of hours to accomplish all that his calendar demanded and still give time to others. His life is best described by the statement, "When you want something done and done well, ask the busiest man you know to do it." That was Mike Ellis.

Printed in the United States
By Bookmasters